The Twisted Sisters
Knit Sweaters

A Knit-to-Fit Workshop

Lynne Vogel

 INTERWEAVE PRESS

Technical editor: Jean Lampe
Photography: Joe Coca

Text © 2007, Lynne Vogel
Photography © 2007, Interweave Press LLC

Interweave Press LLC
201 East Fourth Street
Loveland, Colorado 80537 USA
www.interweave.com

Printed in China
by Asia Pacific Offset

Library of Congress Cataloging-in-
  Publication Data

Vogel, Lynne, 1952-
  The twisted sisters sweater workbook : blueprint for
custom knitting / Lynne Vogel, author.
    p. cm.
  Includes index.
  ISBN 1-931499-69-1 (pbk.)
  1. Sweaters. 2. Knitting--Patterns. 3. Hand spinning.
I. Title.
  TT825.V573 2007
  746.43'20432--dc22
                      2006023457

10 9 8 7 6 5 4 3 2 1

acknowledgments

This book was long in the making. Many heartfelt thanks are in order to all involved.

I can't thank the folks at Interweave Press enough for supporting the conception of the Knitter Fitter. Rebecca Campbell and Marilyn Murphy had the compassion to ease time constraints through the passings of three dearly loved family members. Judith Durant and Jean Lampe flanked me as I wrestled brainchild to paper. Ann Budd championed a dynamic organization, fitting the information like puzzle pieces. Joe Coca took the loveliest photos ever, Gayle Ford and Ann Swanson drew beautiful illustrations, and Paulette Livers laid out one heck of a beautiful book. Many thanks.

Here's a big round of applause for the contributors. Because this book began with enough content to fill three books, much work fell by the wayside. A salute to Rachael, Sue, Ellen (we even knitted over the phone), Elizabeth, Lynn, Jane, and Jeanne, who worked so hard behind the scenes. Kudos to Debby, Crystal, and Mary K for their glorious gallery pieces. Three cheers to our project mavens, Mary P, Linda, Laurie, and the very patient Gail, who waited so long to finally wear that red Aran. Thank you Alina for being my right arm. Thanks and thanks again to Lori L for all your gorgeous work in project and gallery.

And a yippee and yahoo to Twisted Mom Sandy, whose cover sweater rocks! You are a bottomless well of encouragement and inspiration.

There were many guiding lights along the way. Rita, you never doubted me. Mazie, you held a steadfast center. James and Monk, you kept me real. Mom and Mary Willie, you were guardian angels. Blessings to all.

And to my wonderful readers who never stopped pleading for a second book, I can finally say: "Here it is!"

contents

introduction

This book was born at a Twisted Sisters get-together when Lynn Nagasako, our natural-dye queen, asked, "Why don't you write a book about all the different ways to knit the same sweater?"

I've knitted hundreds of sweaters but have never knitted the same one twice. Most of them sprang from the same roots, but something always changed: the yarn, the size, the shape; usually all three. As I spoke with other twisted sisters, I found that as handspinners, most of us had to adapt either our yarn to fit a pattern or the pattern to fit our yarn. So we agreed to meet this challenge: Knit an original sweater by altering a basic drop-shoulder pullover—expand, shrink, shape, and decorate it to meet your practical requirements and express your personal style. The following chapters explore the bare bones required in this challenge: choosing and using yarn, the ins and outs of the basic pattern and details of knitting techniques, and the sweaters we produced.

A Kind of Pattern

Generating instructions for different sizes of the same pattern can cause frustration for the pattern writer. The more complicated the details, the more difficult it is to adapt them to different sizes. This says nothing about the frustration on the reader's end of things. Line-by-line patterns are hard enough to follow with one set of numbers—add extra sizes in parentheses and it's easy to read the wrong number by mistake.

What's more, general sizes such as Small, Medium, and Large represent only a portion of the population. These sizes are often inconsistent, depending on the way a style fits the body. What may be called Large in one style can be smaller than a Small in another. Have you or someone you know ever been "left out" of a really cool pattern because it wasn't sized to fit you? This exclusion is not purposeful, just practical. It's impossible to size for everyone, leaving a large portion of the knitting public to learn how to size, alter, or even design from scratch.

The Knitter Fitter System presented in Chapter Two changes all that. This system allows you to knit a sweater that will fit anyone from a toddler to a sumo wrestler with any yarn you chose. The Classic Crew sweaters in Chapter Three and Chapter Four outline every detail from swatching for gauge to adding finishing touches, whether you want to knit your sweater from the bottom up (or top down) or from side to side. Use the Fitter List to record all the important measurements and their conversions to the number of stitches and/or rows for your gauge. Use the Sweater Map to visualize where each of these measurements goes and how the individual pieces of the sweater fit together.

The Knitter Fitter System is infinitely variable, and some of those variations are outlined in Chapter Five. The projects that follow illustrate how the Twisted Sisters made changes to the length, neckline, and/or shoulders of the Classic Crew to create completely different and unique garments. With a little imagination, you can use these concepts to make any sweater you want in whatever size you want. Say goodbye to Small, Medium, and Large for good.

The tools we outline here may be found in sweater software programs. But sometimes there is no substitute for getting your hands in your work. After all, that's why we knit. The ability to manipulate your ideas with yarn and needles or with a pencil, paper, and eraser can trigger a type of creativity lost to the keyboard and mouse.

A long time ago, a teacher told me to just pick up my needles and start knitting. At the time, my rational brain recoiled, yet my intuitive one strained at the leash. Think of the Knitter Fitter as a safety rope for knitters ready to look over the edge into uncharted realms. Just start knitting and watch your yarn turn into gorgeous sweaters.

Who Are the Twisted Sisters and Friends?

Sandy Sitzman, Twisted Mom and "Millennium Queen Enabler of Prospective and Realized Fiber Enthusiasts," began collecting members for the Portland, Oregon-based spinning group known as Twisted Sisters in the late 1980s. The group made yearly pilgrimages to Eugene's Black Sheep Gathering to spin, knit, and laugh their fool heads off. The hilarity soon spread to the Oregon Coast, NW Wools in Portland, and Dome Central, Sandy's home in Banks. The small, tightly knit group has grown to include a few friends from other states and one nomad who refuses to stay put.

The Twisted Sisters include:

In Alabama:
Mary Kaiser, Birmingham
In California:
Lori Lawson, San Juan Capistrano
Debby Schnabel, Pine Grove
In Oregon:
Linda Berning/NW Wools, Portland
Sue Brooks, Boring
Crystal Buckley, Portland
Alina Egerman, Portland
Ellen Farr, Portland
Gail Marracci, Scappoose
Lynn Nagasako, Portland
Jane Penny, Portland
Jan Prewitt, Portland
Stephanie Prewitt, Portland
Sandy Sitzman, Banks
Laurie Weinsoft, Portland
In Tennessee:
Mary Priestly, Sewanee
Lynne Vogel, Sewanee
In Washington:
Jeanne Roll, Vancouver
Elizabeth Farr, Friday Harbor
In a lot of places:
Rachael Hocking, Banks, Oregon; Dar Es Salaam, Tanzania; Njombe; Tanzania; Multnomah, Oregon; and, most recently, Goldendale, Washington (but not for long).

Chapter One

Yarn and Fabric

What can be more important than a knitter's choice of yarn? Yarn is the fabric of the sweater. Whether a sweater is simple or elaborate, the choice of yarn does more than influence the look and feel; when knitted, it becomes the fabric. Therefore, it is the look and feel.

Because knitted fabric is built from the seemingly nothingness of two sticks and some string, there is a tendency to think of it as something else. When most of us think of fabric, we think of the woven variety, such as shirting, denim, calico, or satin. But think of the wardrobe-staple T-shirt made from knitted fabric—these stitches may appear too small to be knitted by hand, but they could be.

Even knitters who follow patterns to the letter using the suggested yarn, needles, and stitch pattern are creating their own fabric. They have the additional advantage that they can guide every detail of that fabric and the fit of the garment it produces.

The variety of yarns and patterns currently available is overwhelming. New yarn stores are popping up everywhere—each one a treasure trove of enticing colors, fibers, and designs. Artisan yarns are widely available on the Internet and at fiber fairs nationwide. Everywhere you turn, it seems you're faced with a beautiful new yarn. But not all yarns are appropriate for all projects. Before you settle on a yarn for your next project, take into account the type of yarn, how it knits up, and how you want the finished garment to look and feel.

Yarn Classification

Yarns are most commonly classified by weight, which is a measure of the thickness of the yarn. This weight influences how many stitches and rows of stitches constitute an inch of knitted fabric. In order of increasing thickness, the standard yarn weights are lace or fingering, sport, DK, worsted, chunky, and bulky. The table below shows how the Craft Yarn Council of America has classified these yarn weights according to the number of stitches expected per inch of knitting on specific needle sizes.

Yarn can also be classified by grist—the amount of fiber required to make a certain thickness of yarn, reported as wraps per inch (WPI). Wraps per inch is a measure of the width of a particular yarn, based on the number of strands that fit side by side in one inch. The easiest way to determine WPI is to wrap the yarn around a narrow rod or ruler for one inch. The heavier the yarn, the fewer number of wraps in one inch; the finer the yarn, the more wraps. Like yarn weight, WPI relates to the number of stitches expected per inch of knitting, but because it is a measurement of the actual size of the yarn, it provides a more accurate idea of the expected gauge and needle size. Some knitting books and magazines include WPI information along with general weight classifications.

When determining WPI, be sure to acknowledge the loft of the yarn by wrapping loosely so that each wrap just touches the last. Depending on the fiber content, the yarn construction, and the tension with which the yarn is wrapped, some yarns may compact when they are wrapped around the needle but fluff up once the stitches slide off the needles—WPI should reflect this quality of the yarn.

Although yarn weight and WPI fundamentally suggest a well-balanced gauge and needle size, don't be afraid to deviate from these guidelines. By simply changing the needle size, you can make a fabric that's elegantly drapey or serviceably dense. Use the table on page 9 to help you decide the combination of yarn weight, yardage per pound, WPI, needle size, and gauge needed to create the fabric you want.

Follow the recommendations for "Pliable or Normal Fabric" for a fabric that is flexible without being too dense or too open (see Mary's Classic Crew on page 15). When held up to the light, the stitches in this type of fabric will touch each other but allow light to shine through. This fabric is reasonably durable and well suited for sweaters, vests, and other indoor garments. For outerwear, it offers only moderate wind resistance.

Follow the recommendations for "Drapey or Openwork Fabric" to create a fabric that's pleasantly pliable and

The Craft Yarn Council of America (CYCA) has devised a standard numbering system for reporting yarn weights. This system is used for the projects in this book.

STANDARD YARN WEIGHT SYSTEM						
Yarn Weight Symbol and Category Name	**1** SUPER FINE	**2** FINE	**3** LIGHT	**4** MEDIUM	**5** BULKY	**6** SUPER BULKY
Type of Yarns in Category	Sock, Fingering, Baby	Sport, Baby	DK, Light Worsted	Worsted, Afghan, Aran	Chunky, Craft, Rug	Bulky, Roving
*Knitted Gauge Range in Stockinette Stitch to 4" (10 cm)	27–32 sts	23–26 sts	21–24 sts	16–20 sts	12–15 sts	6–11 sts
Recommended Needle in Metric Size Range	2.25–3.25 mm	3.25–3.75 mm	3.75–4.5 mm	4.5–5.5 mm	5.5–8 mm	8 mm and larger
Recommended Needle in U.S. Size Range	1–3	3–5	5–7	7–9	9–11	11 and larger

*Guidelines Only: The above reflect the most commonly used gauges and needles for specific yarn categories.

To measure WPI, count the number of wraps in one inch.

drapey (see Angel Wing Lace Float on page 104). When held up to the light, the stitches in this fabric will barely touch each other and will allow a lot of light to shine through. This fabric is somewhat sheer, not particularly durable, and easily snagged. But it is very light and comfortable to wear. It is commonly used for shawls, scarves, and lightweight layered garments. This type of fabric offers minimal warmth and no wind resistance.

Follow the recommendations for "Dense or Stiff Fabric" to create a fabric that's stiff and not particularly flexible (see Alina's Basketweave Coat, page 53). When held up to the light, the stitches in this fabric are tightly packed together and allow very little light to shine through. This fabric is very durable and great for rugs, purses, and totes. Dense fabrics knitted with finer yarns are ideal for socks, mittens, fitted vests, and coats. They are very warm regardless of the yarn used and as wind resistant as knitted fabrics can be.

Gauge: The Key to Success

Gauge—the number of stitches and rows per inch of knitting—is the key to successful knitting. An understanding of gauge will unlock the door to fit, yarn substitution, and pattern alteration. If you want to knit a piece of cloth to particular dimensions (as in a sweater that fits), you must knit to a specific gauge. The only way to know in advance that you're knitting to the right gauge is to knit a sample swatch. There is no alternative. Every yarn, every pair of needles, and every knitter has idiosyncrasies that affect gauge. The only way to discover how these variables interact is to knit a sample.

To get an accurate gauge, knit a swatch with the needles and in the stitch pattern you intend to use for your project. Different types of needles and different stitch patterns will produce different gauges. Don't skimp here—you'll get the best gauge measurement from a large swatch that allows you to measure at least four inches each horizontally (stitch gauge) and vertically (row gauge) without interference from irregular edge stitches, distortion from cast-on or bind-off rows, or draw-in from the last row of stitches on the needles. Loosely bind off the last row of stitches or slip them off the needle (and onto waste yarn) before measuring the gauge, unless your swatch is so long that there's plenty of fabric to measure that isn't anywhere near the needles.

If you're short on yarn for your swatch, use a provisional cast-on (see Glossary, page 134), knit at least 2½" square, and slip the last row of stitches onto waste yarn. Because the cast-on and bind-off edges are as flexible as the knitting, this allows you to get an accurate measurement on fewer stitches.

It is important to swatch in the round if you intend to knit your garment in the round. (Don't confuse knitting back and forth on circular needles with knitting in the round. Knitting in the round is when you join your knitting and knit in a circular fashion, with every row being worked in the same direction.) Many knitters knit tighter than they purl, or vice versa. When working stockinette stitch in the round, every stitch is knitted every row. If you knit tighter than you purl, your gauge will be tighter when you work in rounds than when you work in rows with the same yarn and needles. Even if the difference is only a quarter of a stitch every 4", it can add up to several inches over the circumference of a sweater.

To get an accurate gauge for knitting in the round, knit a tube using a set of double-pointed needles or a very short circular needle. Another option is to knit a

Yarn Weight	Yards per Pound	Wraps per Inch (WPI)	DRAPEY OR OPENWORK FABRIC (most usually recommended)		PLIABLE OR NORMAL FABRIC (most usually recommended)		DENSE OR STIFF FABRIC (most usually recommended)	
			Recommended Gauge in St. st per Inch	US Needle Size	Recommended Gauge in St. st per Inch	US Needle Size	Recommended Gauge in St. st per Inch	US Needle Size
Bulky	400 yards or less	8 wraps or less	2 sts per inch	15–17	2–3 sts per inch	11 13	3½ sts per inch	10
Chunky	600–800 yards	10 wraps	3 sts	13	3–4 sts	10–11	4½ sts	7
Worsted	900–1200 yards	12 wraps	3¼ sts	11	4½ sts	8–9	5½	4
DK	1100–1400 yards	13 wraps	4½ sts	8	5 sts	6–7	6½ sts	2
Sport	1200–1800 yards	14 wraps	5 sts	7	5–6 sts	4–6	8 sts	1
Fingering to Laceweight	1900 or finer	16 wraps or more	5½–6 sts	5–6	8 + sts	3 or smaller	10 or more	00–0

flat swatch. Using double-pointed or circular needles, knit every row with the same side of the swatch facing you, stranding the yarn across the back so that each row begins with the same stitch. Be careful to carry the strand loosely across the back of the work so that it doesn't cause the knitting to pucker. Measure the gauge in the center portion of the swatch as far from the edge stitches as possible—the edge stitches will be affected by the loose strand connecting them and will not reflect the true gauge.

Before measuring, lightly block the sample by covering it with a barely damp cloth and gently steaming it with an iron. Note that although this process is recommended for natural fibers, it usually isn't necessary (or desirable) with synthetic yarns.

Measure the number of stitches in 4", including partial stitches, both vertically and horizontally. Divide this number by four to determine the gauge per inch. Be sure to take partial stitches into account—again, one-fourth of a stitch difference every 4" can add up to several inches in the circumference of a sweater.

It's easy to see and count the number of stitches per inch on a white or solid-colored smooth yarn by placing a ruler on top of the sample and counting the stitches along one row. This can become more of a challenge with variegated and textured yarns. When it's difficult to see the individual stitches, determine the gauge by using simple math. Keep track of the number of stitches cast-on for the sample swatch and the number of rows knitted. To measure the stitch gauge, place a straight pin after the first stitch and before the last stitch of a row. Place your ruler along one row of the swatch and measure the width between the pins. Divide the number of stitches between the pins by the number of inches between the pins. To get the row gauge, place pins horizontally in the swatch just inside the cast-on and bind-off rows. Place your ruler along the vertical stitch line and measure the length of the swatch between the pins. Divide the number of rows between the pins by the number of inches between the pins.

Measure the number of stitches over four inches.

Knitting with Variegated Yarns

The Twisted Sisters love working with color, and one of our favorite ways to incorporate lots of color is to use handpainted and variegated yarn. Most of us like to dye our own yarns, but if dyeing isn't for you, you can purchase a wide array of handpainted and variegated yarns from commercial or independent yarn producers (see Resources, page 142, for a few).

Handpainted and variegated handspun yarns form stripes of color when knitted. The length of the color bands will determine how those stripes will appear in the knitted fabric. One inch of knitting, regardless of gauge, will take about 3" to 4" of yarn, depending on the stitch pattern—heavily cabled knitting takes more; slip-stitch and color patterns take a little less. But as a rule of thumb, a $3^1/_2$" color band will knit up into a 1" width of stitches.

Yarns that have long color bands will produce varying widths of stripes over the standard width of an adult sweater. The same yarn knitted in narrow panels or areas of intarsia or entrelac will produce solid colors and gradations of color depending on the colorway of the yarn and the lengths of the color bands. Color bands an inch or shorter in length will show up as dots when knitted.

No matter the length of the color bands, handpainted yarn usually develops a distinct color pattern repeat when knitted. This repeat isn't usually exactly the same for each skein of

Left: variegated yarn before and after reskeining. Right: knitted fabric.

A swatch of handpainted brushed mohair from Dicentra Designs is raveled to show the difference in the length of color bands before and after knitting.

handpainted yarn, so don't expect every skein to knit up exactly the same. To minimize the difference between different skeins, alternate knitting two rows from one skein with two rows from another, as in the Bouclé Boat Neck on page 48. If the skeins are very different, alternate two rows each from three different skeins.

Another way to distribute variations is to knit with two strands of yarn held together. Double stranding is a beautiful way to "paint" with yarn, especially finer yarns. Alternate one strand at a time as above while carrying the other strand twice as far. For example, if you have three skeins, A, B and C, knit two rows with A and B held together, followed by two rows with B and C held together, followed by two rows with C and A held together, and so on.

Some skeins may have an obviously longer section of one color than the others. Rather than trying to disperse this difference over the entire sweater, group the accent skeins in a single area as a design element, such as at the collar and cuffs.

Yardage: How Much Yarn Will You Need?

Figuring yardage is not an exact science. A conservative ballpark figure plus at least 10 percent usually works. If you are designing as you go, get plenty of yarn or fiber. You may not be able to get more later.

Gauge (the number of stitches and rows per inch of knitting) is probably the most important factor in determining the amount of yarn you'll need. The smaller the gauge, the more rows you'll knit, the more yarn you'll need—it's that simple.

To get a rough estimate of how much you'll need, flip through knitting magazines and highlight the gauges and number of yards in each project to get a good idea of the range of yardage necessary. For example, a classic stockinette crew-neck sweater like Mary's Classic Crew (page 15) knitted at $4\frac{1}{2}$ stitches per inch on size 8 needles can take anywhere from 1,100 to 1,300 yards, depending on the stretchiness of the yarn. Pay attention to the stitch patterns, too. Heavy cable patterns take about half again as much yarn as the same size sweater knitted in stockinette stitch. Sweaters knitted with color stranding take roughly half again as much yardage for each row of stranding.

Most yarn shop workers will usually have a good idea about how much you'll need of the yarns they carry, even if you don't have a specific pattern in mind. But be considerate when seeking help from yarn shops—don't ask for more help than you're willing to return in the form of purchases.

For a more accurate estimate of yardage needs, you'll have to do some math. But don't worry—this is really pretty easy. Measure about 10 yards of yarn and place a small safety pin through the yarn to mark each yard. Use this yarn to knit a swatch that measures exactly 4" square, removing the pins as you come to them. Chances are, you'll finish your swatch in between a pair of pins. Estimate how much of that

yard you used. For example, if 2 feet of yarn remain before the next pin, you've used $\frac{1}{3}$ of a yard. Count the number of pins you removed as you knitted and add the partial yard measurement at the end to determine how many yards of yarn you use to knit the 4"-square swatch (which translates to 16 square inches of fabric). Next, make a generous determination of how many square inches of fabric are in the sweater you want to make (remember to include collars and edgings).

To do this, make a scale drawing of your sweater on graph paper. Draw the bodice back, the bodice front, and one sleeve. Split the other sleeve lengthwise in two halves and draw each half next to the first sleeve to make two rectangles. Multiply the width of

each rectangle by its length to get a good approximation of the number of square inches in your sweater. For the example here, the front and back take 56" x 26"=1,456 square inches; the two sleeves take 28" x 15"=420 square inches.

Divide the number of square inches just determined for your sweater by the number of square inches in your swatch (16 square inches in our 4" square example) to determine how many swatches it would take to make your sweater. Multiply that number by the number of yards knitted into your swatch to determine the minimum number of yards you'll need. For a safety margin, add 10 percent to this number.

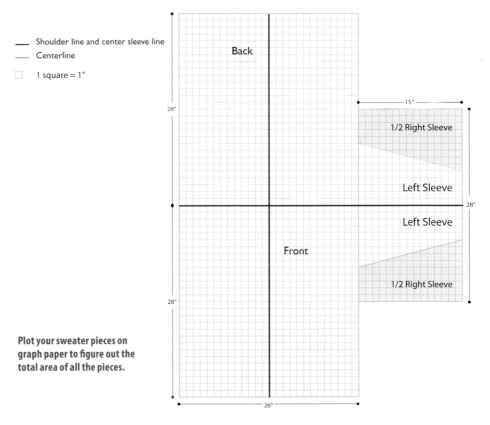

—— Shoulder line and center sleeve line
—— Centerline
☐ 1 square = 1"

Plot your sweater pieces on graph paper to figure out the total area of all the pieces.

Chapter Two

The Knitter Fitter System

All of the projects in this book are based on a two-part Knitter Fitter System: the Fitter List and the Sweater Map. The Fitter List is a record of key sweater measurements and their translations into numbers of stitches and rows of knitting. The Sweater Map is an illustration of how the individual sweater pieces fit together. This system is infinitely versatile and variable—if you can read a tape measure, you can design your own sweater.

When I knitted my first sweater, I worked all the pieces from the bottom up. For a long time I thought that was the only way to knit a sweater. As my knitting skills improved, however, I realized I could knit from the top down just as easily or that I could orient my rows lengthwise and knit from side to side. It wasn't long before I tried combining different knitting directions in a single sweater.

No matter which direction you want to knit your sweater, it's an easy matter of taking a few body measurements (or measurements of a sweater that fits the way you like) to customize the fit. From there, it's only a matter of adding or subtracting inches from that sweater to achieve any style you want—from form fitting to oversized, from cropped to coat length. From there, it's a simple matter of knitting a generous swatch and taking accurate stitch- and row-gauge measurements, and using these measurements to design every aspect of a sweater, whether you want to knit that sweater from the bottom up (or from the top down) or from side to side.

The Fitter List

The Fitter List includes key measurements and the numbers of stitches and rows that correspond to these measurements (based on your gauge swatch). At first glance, this looks like an impossible amount of information. But don't despair—you only need to determine the bodice width and length before you start knitting. All the other numbers will be added one at a time as you knit. This approach allows you to determine things such as armhole depth, neckline shape, and sleeve dimensions based on the hand, drape, and stretch of your particular knitted fabric. And when you're done knitting, you'll have a complete record of every decision you made along the way so you can knit another sweater just like it. Or, even better, use this information as a basis for making successful changes in fit or design for a completely different sweater.

The Fitter List

Measure your body and allow for the appropriate amount of ease (see page 14) or measure a sweater that fits the way you like and enter the numbers below. Refer to your gauge swatch for your stitch and row gauges, then translate each measurement into numbers of stitches and/or rows as you go along. Note that the direction you knit the sweater pieces (up and down or side to side) will determine whether you follow the stitch or row numbers (you only need to fill in the appropriate blank).

Yarn

Yarn name:_____

Fiber content:_____

Weight classification:_____WPI:_____Yards/pounds used:_____

Gauge

Stitches per inch:_____Rows per inch:_____Needle size:_____

Details

Cast-on method: _____

Bind-off method: _____

Selvedge treatment: _____

Sleeve increase/decrease method: _____

Seam technique:_____

Notes/Variations

Note any variations you make to the basic pattern here.

_____

_____

_____

_____

_____

_____

_____

_____

_____

Sweater Measurements

Bodice

Circumference:_____inches; _____stitches; _____rows

Width:_____inches; _____stitches; _____rows

Cast-On Stitches:_____stitches (includes edge stitches)

Length With Edging:_____inches, _____stitches; _____rows

Length Without Edging:_____inches; _____stitches; _____rows

Length of Lower Edging:_____inches; _____stitches; _____rows

Armhole Depth:_____inches; _____stitches; _____rows

Back Neck Width Without Edging:_____inches; _____stitches; _____rows

Back Neck Width With Edging:_____inches; _____stitches; _____rows

Front Neck Depth Without Edging:_____inches; _____stitches; _____rows

Front Neck Depth With Edging:_____inches; _____stitches; _____rows

Neckline Edging: _____inches; _____stitches; _____rows

Lower Front Neck Width: _____stitches; _____rows

Begin Front Neck At: _____stitches; _____rows

Shoulder Width: _____stitches; _____rows

Sleeves

Sleeve Length Without Edging:_____inches; _____stitches; _____rows

Sleeve Length With Edging:_____inches; _____stitches; _____rows

Cuff Circumference:_____inches; _____stitches; _____rows

Half Cuff Circumference: _____inches; _____stitches; _____rows

Cuff Length:_____inches; _____stitches; _____rows

Upper Arm Circumference:_____inches; _____stitches; _____rows

Half Upper Arm Circumference:_____inches; _____stitches; _____rows

Sleeve Taper Rate:_____stitches decreased/increased every _____rows; _____times

Cardigan (page 37) • Neck Variations (page 38) • Shoulder Variations (page 40) • Sleeve Variations (page 42) • Edgings (page 44)

The Sweater Map

The Sweater Map is a bird's-eye-view of all of the sweater pieces before they are sewn together. This at-a-glance overview lets you conceptualize the sweater before you begin knitting and provides a foundation for making additions and alterations along the way or for future sweaters. Annotate the map with arrows to indicate knitting direction, stitch and row counts to indicate where and how neck and sleeve shaping takes place, and notes about design details such as collar and edging choices, and you'll have a complete picture of your sweater.

To draw your map in perfect proportion, plot your measurements on ordinary graph paper at a scale of one inch to one square. You can make custom print-able PDF files of any size graph paper by visiting the Web (see page 142). You can also plot your measure-ments actual size on pellon yardage (see page 46).

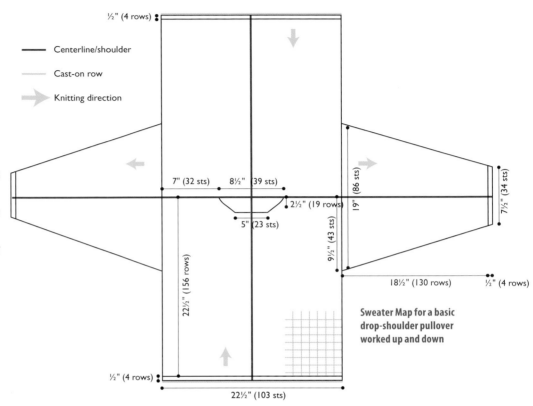

— Centerline/shoulder
— Cast-on row
→ Knitting direction

½" (4 rows)
7" (32 sts)   8½" (39 sts)
2½" (19 rows)
5" (23 sts)
19" (86 sts)
7½" (34 sts)
9½" (43 rows)
22½" (156 rows)
18½" (130 rows)   ½" (4 rows)
½" (4 rows)
22½" (103 sts)

Sweater Map for a basic drop-shoulder pullover worked up and down

Sweater Sizing

Deciding on the right size for a sweater is a relative thing. It is determined as much by style and fit as actual body measure-ments. Use your actual measurements as a foundation, then add (or subtract) inches to achieve the fit you want.

Close Fit or Fitted: The garment chest measurement is the same as your body chest measurement. If a fabric is very stretchy and is meant to fit very snugly, then measure the fabric while it is stretched the desired amount.

Add less than 2"–4" to your actual body measurement for a close fit.

Standard or Classic: The garment chest measurement is a bit larger than the body chest measurement. This larger measurement allows for more ease of movement and is appropriately called "ease."

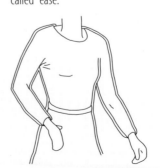

Add about 2–4" to your actual body measurement for a standard fit.

Loose or Oversized: The garment chest measurement is four or more inches larger than the actual chest measurement. Lots of ease!

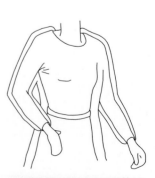

Add 4" or more to your actual body measurement for a loose fit.

Chapter Three

Up-and-Down Construction

In a sweater that is knitted up and down, the pieces are worked from the hem upward to the neck or from the neck downward to the hem. In either case, the rows of knitting run perpendicular to the center line of the bodice or sleeve. When broken down into individual steps, it's surprisingly easy to design and knit a drop-shoulder sweater in this orientation. The instructions here are for working the front and back upward from the hem to the neck, and the sleeves either upward from the cuff to the shoulder or downward from the shoulder to the cuff. For our example, we'll use a classic crew pullover knitted by Mary Priestly.

$\mathcal{T}$he Fitter List for Drop-Shoulder Sweater Knitted Up and Down (Mary's Classic Crew)

Measure your body and allow for the appropriate amount of ease (see page 14) or measure a sweater that fits the way you like and enter the numbers below. Refer to your gauge swatch for your stitch and row gauges, then translate each measurement into numbers of stitches and/or rows as you go along.

Yarn

Yarn name: **Ashland Bay Trader's Falkland's Superwash**

Fiber content: **100% Superwash Wool**

Weight classification: **Worsted (#4 Medium)**

WPI: **11**

Number of yards/pounds used: **1,180 yards; 15½ ounces**

Gauge

Stitches per inch: **4½** Rows per inch: **7** Needle size: **US 8 (5mm)**

Details

Cast-on method: **Loop**

Bind-off method: **Chain**

Selvedge treatment: **Chain stitch**

Sleeve increase/decrease method: **Paired decreases**

Seam technique: **Mattress stitch**

Notes/Variations

Mary wanted to make the decreases on right-side rows only, so she used a taper of *6, 4. The first set of paired decreases was made on the 6th row, the next pair of decreases was made 4 rows after that; the 6, 4 sequence was repeated from * 12 more times to complete the total number of decreases.

Sweater Measurements

Bodice

Circumference: **45** inches

Width: **22½** inches; **101** stitches

Cast-On Stitches: **103** stitches (includes edge stitches)

Length With Edging: **23** inches; **160** rows

Length Without Edging: **22½** inches; **156** rows

Length of Lower Edging: **½** inches; **4** rows

Armhole Depth: **9½** inches; **66** rows

Back Neck Width Without Edging: **8½** inches; **39** stitches

Back Neck Width With Edging: **7½** inches; **33** stitches

Front Neck Depth Without Edging: **2½** inches; **18** rows

Front Neck Depth With Edging: **1½** inches

Neckline Edging: **4** rows

Lower Front Neck Width: **5** stitches

Begin Front Neck At: **20½** inches

Shoulder Width: **7** inches; **32** stitches

Sleeves

Sleeve Length Without Edging: **18½** inches; **130** rows

Sleeve Length With Edging: **19** inches; **134** rows

Cuff Circumference: **7½** inches; **34** stitches

Half Cuff Circumference: **3¾** inches; **17** stitches

Cuff Length: **½** inches; ___ stitches; **4** rows

Upper Arm Circumference: **19** inches; **86** stitches

Half Upper Arm Circumference: **9½** inches; **43** stitches

Sleeve Taper Rate: **2** stitches decreased every **5** rows **26** times; **130** rows

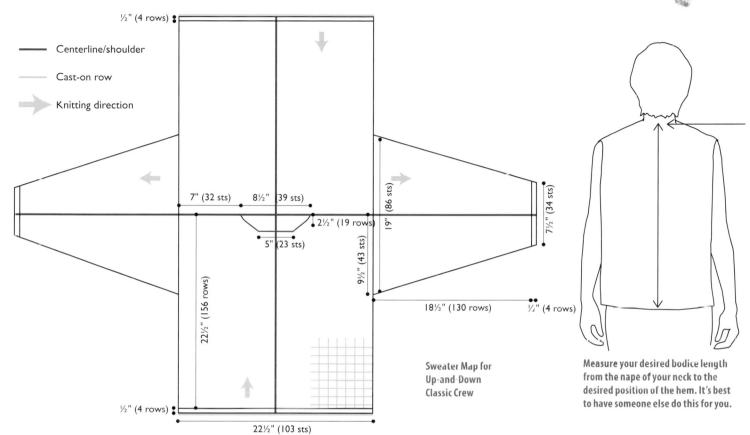

½" (4 rows)

Centerline/shoulder
Cast-on row
Knitting direction

7" (32 sts) 8½" (39 sts)

2½" (19 rows)

5" (23 sts)

19" (86 sts)

7½" (34 sts)

9½" (43 sts)

22½" (156 rows)

18½" (130 rows) ½" (4 rows)

Sweater Map for
Up-and-Down
Classic Crew

½" (4 rows)

22½" (103 sts)

Measure your desired bodice length
from the nape of your neck to the
desired position of the hem. It's best
to have someone else do this for you.

1 Determine Gauge

Using the yarn, needles, and stitch pattern you plan to use for your sweater, knit a generous sample swatch to determine stitch and row gauge (Chapter One, page 8). Enter this information for Gauge in the Fitter List.

2 Determine Bodice Circumference and Length

Using a tape measure, measure your body circumference at your chest, waist, and hips. Use the largest of these measurements for your torso measurement. Add the desired amount of ease to this body measurement (Chapter One, page 14)—0–2" for a close fit, about 2–4" for a standard fit, or 4" or more for an oversized fit. Enter this

number for Bodice Circumference in the Fitter List. Divide this number by two for the Bodice Width.

Alternatively, measure a shirt or sweater that fits the way you like, ideally one that has a drop-shoulder construction. Lay the garment on a flat surface and measure the width. Enter this number for Bodice Width in the Fitter List. Double this number for the Bodice Circumference.

To determine the sweater length, ask a friend to measure you from your shoulder line straight down the center of your back to where you want the hem to fall. Alternatively, measure the length (from shoulder seam at the neckline to hem) of a sweater that's the length you want. Enter this number for Bodice Length With Edging in the Fitter List. Decide how much of this length you'll want to devote to edging and enter this number for Length of Lower Edging. Subtract Length of Lower Edging from Bodice Length With Edging and enter this number for Bodice Length Without Edging.

3 Determine Stitch Count

Multiply your stitch gauge by your desired bodice circumference to determine the number of stitches you'll need to make the bodice the size you want. Mary had a stitch gauge of $4^1/2$ stitches per inch. She wanted a circumference of 45" for a standard, comfortable fit. Mary therefore needed 202.5 stitches (4.5 stitches per inch x 45 inches = 202.5 stitches). Mary rounded this down to 202 stitches. Divide this number by two to determine the number of stitches for just the bodice back (or the bodice front). For Mary, this was 101 stitches. If you want to add selvedge stitches (see below) to facilitate seaming later, add them to this number. Enter the total number of stitches in the Fitter List for Cast-On Stitches.

Mary wanted to use a chain selvedge and sew the seams with a mattress stitch 1 stitch from each selvedge edge. This meant that she'd lose the equivalent of 4 stitches total in the side seams, which translates to almost 1" in the total finished circumference at Mary's gauge of

$4^1/2$ stitches per inch. To make up for this difference, Mary decided to add an extra stitch at each selvedge edge, so she increased her cast-on number to 103 stitches. If Mary had been working with a finer yarn whose selvedge stitches added up to ½" or less of width, or if she had chosen a different selvedge/seam combination, she might have chosen not to add these extra stitches.

Multiply your row gauge by the desired bodice length to determine the number of rows you'll need to work. At this point, this number is only a guideline—you can always adjust the number of rows later if you want to fine-tune the length.

4 Knit the Bodice Back

Using the method of your choice (Glossary, pages 131–132), cast on the desired number of stitches. Work the edging of your choice for the desired length (Mary worked knit 1, purl 1 rib for 4 rows), then work your chosen stitch pattern (Mary used stockinette stitch) until the piece measures about 3" above the edging. Lay the piece on a flat surface and measure the width to confirm it's the size you intended. If the piece is not the correct width, remeasure your gauge, recalculate the number of stitches to cast on, and reknit the piece to this point. Once you're

$\mathcal{S}$elvedge Stitches

In knitting, the selvedges are the first and last stitch of each row, and they are incorporated into the seams when the pieces are sewn together (there are no selvedge stitches in pieces knitted in the round). There are a number of different ways to work selvedge stitches (see Glossary, page 139), and the way you choose can greatly facilitate working seams (or picking up stitches) later. Different types of selvedge stitches work best with different types of seaming stitches, so you'll want to decide on the type of selvedge stitches and seams in

the early stages of your design process.

Some types of seams cause the selvedge stitches to turn into the seam allowance. If you don't allow for these stitches to be "lost" in the seams, the finished dimensions of your sweater, especially one knitted with bulky yarn, can be 1" (or more) smaller than you calculated. Other types of seams can be worked with the knitted pieces butted up against one another without any overlap. These types of seams don't affect the finished dimensions of garments.

Knitters often complain about having to sew seams (and we show several ways to avoid seaming in your projects). But more often than not, it's not the process of sewing seams that's problematic, it's the fact that the selvedge edges are uneven and the knitters are having trouble seeing where to guide the seaming needle. If you pay attention to selvedges as you are knitting, they will be easier to see when it comes time to sew, and the task will not seem so distasteful.

satisfied that the width is correct, continue to work in your chosen stitch pattern until the piece measures the desired Bodice Length With Edging.

At this point, you can fine-tune the length by holding the piece (while it's still on the needles) against your body. While standing up, center the knitting on your body, holding the needles even with the top of your shoulders. Allowing the piece to hang naturally, confirm that you like where the lower edge falls. It's an easy matter to add or subtract rows at this point to get exactly the length you want, but if you do make adjustments, be sure to update the information on the Fitter List.

Once you've reached the desired length, use the method of your choice (Glossary, pages 131–132) to loosely bind off the stitches. Mary used a simple loop bind-off.

Casting On and Binding Off

The first and last rows of any piece of knitting are just as important as all the rows in between. Even though the techniques of casting on and binding off are different, they serve the same function: to create a stable edge that won't ravel. These rows can be finished edges that stand alone; they can become incorporated into a seam; they can become an invisible part of the fabric when grafted together. There are dozens of ways to cast on and bind off stitches and the methods to choose depend on the look and function you want.

You can choose cast-ons and bind-offs that mirror each other so that the edges have the same look and feel. For example, there are loop, chain, and cable methods of casting on that have corresponding techniques for binding off. When you pair them in a sweater, you'll be hard pressed to say which is the cast-on and which is the bind-off edge. See pages 132–134 of the Glossary for a variety of cast-ons and pages 131–132 for bind-offs.

> *Tip* **Adding Stitch Patterns**
>
> If you wish to knit this sweater with a repeating stitch pattern, you may need to adjust your cast-on number to accommodate full pattern repeats and to center the pattern.
>
> If you plan to add an edging such as ribbing or lace later, subtract the number of inches in your desired edging from the overall bodice length.

5 Determine Front Neckline Width and Depth

You'll use the knitted Bodice Back to map out the exact number of stitches and rows involved in the neck opening on the Bodice Front. First, find the center line of the knitted Bodice Back. If you worked on an even number of stitches, the center line will be the space between 2 stitches. Mark this line with a vertical pin. If you worked on an odd number of stitches, the center line will be an entire stitch. Place a vertical pin on each side of the center stitch.

Standing in front of a mirror, hold the Bodice Back against your body, aligning the centerline of the bodice with the centerline of your body. With straight or safety pins, pin the shoulder edges of the Bodice Back (without stretching or pulling the piece) to the shoulder lines of the shirt you're wearing, leaving the center part unpinned to suggest the desired neck width. This will give you a good idea of how the finished sweater will hang.

> *Tip* **Loose Bind-Off**
>
> A loose bind-off tension will ensure a nonbinding neck and shoulder seams. To ensure that the bind-off is sufficiently loose, knit the last row on needles one size larger, then use the larger needle's mate to work the bind-off row.

Mark the desired finished neck width on each side of the center with vertically placed bobby pins. Mark the desired finished neck depth on the center line with a horizontally placed bobby pin. Be sure not to pin through to your shirt.

Remove the Bodice Back from your shirt and lay it on a flat surface. With a ruler or tape measure, measure the neck width between the vertical pins and enter this number in the Fitter List for Back Neck Width With Edging. Count the number of stitches between the pins and enter this number as well. Measure the neck depth from the shoulder line to the marking pin and enter this number for Front Neck Depth With Edging. Count the number of rows between the shoulder line and marking pin, round up or down to achieve an even number, and enter this number as well.

Chart the Neckline on Graph Paper

Once you know how wide and deep you want your neckline in terms of rows and stitches, you can detail the exact shape on graph paper, allowing each square of the graph paper to represent one stitch. If possible, use knitter's proportional graph paper (Resources, page 142) so the shape you draw will match the shape you'll knit.

First, draw a horizontal line to represent the shoulder line. Bisect this with a vertical line to represent the center front. If you worked the bodice on an even number of stitches, draw the center line on the vertical line of the graph paper. If you worked on an odd number of stitches (as Mary did), shade in a vertical column of squares to represent the center front stitch. Draw a dashed horizontal line at the desired finished neckline depth. This represents the neckline after the ribbing has been added. Mary wanted a finished neckline depth of 2", which translates to 14 rows at her gauge of 7 rows to the inch. Next, account for the depth of neckline ribbing by drawing another horizontal line the appropriate number of rows below for the neckline depth without ribbing. Mary wanted 4 rows

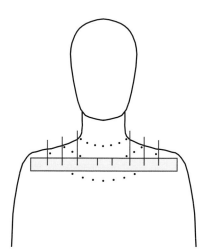

The dotted lines indicate a few possible necklines.

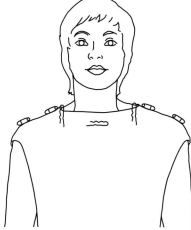

Pin the Bodice Back to the shirt you're wearing and mark the desired neckline width and depth with bobby pins.

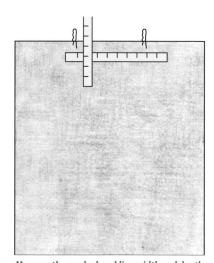

Measure the marked neckline width and depth and translate these measurements to stitches and rows. Plot this shaping onto graph paper.

of ribbing, which translates to about $1/2$". Mary's total neck depth (before ribbing) is therefore 18 rows (14 rows plus 4 rows). Enter this number of rows in the Fitter List for Front Neck Depth Without Edging.

Next, mark the desired finished back neck width along the horizontal shoulder line, centered about the center line. Mary wanted a Back Neck Width With Edging of $7^{1}/2$", which at her gauge, translates to 33.75 stitches. Because Mary has an odd number of stitches to begin with, she rounded this down to 33 stitches. To allow for the $1/2$" neckband, Mary needed to allow $8^{1}/2$" for the Back Neck Width Without Edging, which translates to 38.25 stitches. Mary rounded this up to 39 stitches. Mark the slope between the back and front neck by drawing lines from the edges of the back neck width (without edging) to the front neck depth (without edging). Draw these as jagged lines, working down 2 rows, then toward the center line

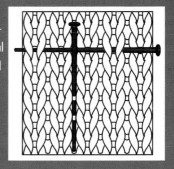

Tip Measuring Knitting
Use a pair of crossed pins to mark a particular point on your knitting. Place a vertical pin parallel to the ladder or stitch line and a horizontal pin parallel to the row line to mark a beginning stitch. The point where the pins cross marks the exact point from which you can measure in either a horizontal or vertical direction.

1 stitch, until you reach the line marking the neck depth (without edging). These lines represent a 1-stitch decrease for every 2 rows of knitting, which produces a nice, rounded neck. Count the number of stitches that remain between the jagged lines on the neck depth (23 stitches in Mary's case) and enter this number in the Fitter List for Lower Front Neck Width.

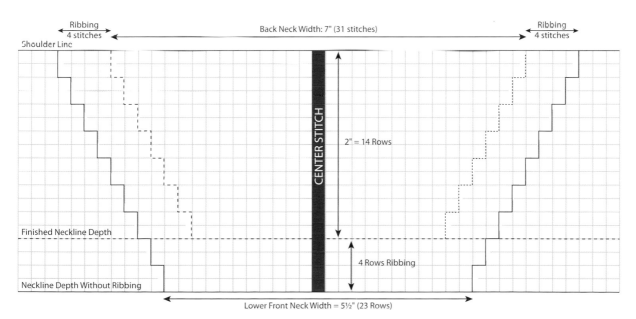

Each square of the neckline chart represents 1 stitch. The lower neck edge is shaped by binding off stitches; the sides are shaped by working single decreases every 2 rows.

6 Knit the Bodice Front

Knit the Bodice Front just like the Bodice Back up to where the neckline shaping begins. To determine where to begin the neckline, subtract the number of rows in Front Neck Depth Without Edging (18 rows in Mary's case) from the number of rows for Bodice Length (160 rows in Mary's case). When you get to this point, mark the center front stitch (or each side of the center front stitch if you're working on an odd number of stitches) with a safety pin or removable stitch marker. This corresponds to the center stitch on your neckline graph. Count the number of stitches on each side of the center stitch to where the neckline shaping begins and mark these with additional markers. Mary had 23 stitches at the base of her neckline, which leaves 40 stitches on each side, given Mary's total stitch count of 103 stitches. You can bind off the center stitches or place them on a holder to incorporate later into the ribbing. Following the neckline graph, work each side of the front neck separately, shaping it by decreasing 1 stitch (k2tog or ssk) at the center front edge every other row (see About Decreases box on page 23) until you reach the total number of rows in the Bodice Length With

Edging. Mary worked k2tog decreases on one side and ssk decreases on the other until she reached a total of 160 rows. Enter the number of stitches remaining in the Fitter List for Shoulder Width. For Mary's sweater, 32 stitches remained for each shoulder after the neckline graph was completed. Bind off the remaining stitches.

Gently steam-block the pieces unless you're working with a synthetic fiber such as nylon that doesn't require blocking.

7 Determine Sleeve Dimensions

Now you're ready to begin the sleeves. First, you'll need to measure the desired armhole depth, sleeve length from cuff to armhole, and cuff circumference. Although you can take these measurements on your body or from a sweater that fits the way you like, you'll get much better results if you take them with respect to the pieces you've already knitted. Knitted fabric has drape and the amount of drape is a factor of your yarn and gauge. One fabric may drape farther off the shoulders than another fabric, and that will determine how wide and how long you'll want to make the sleeves.

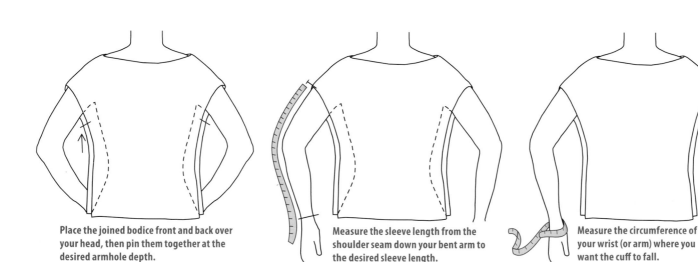

Place the joined bodice front and back over your head, then pin them together at the desired armhole depth.

Measure the sleeve length from the shoulder seam down your bent arm to the desired sleeve length.

Measure the circumference of your wrist (or arm) where you want the cuff to fall.

Armhole Depth

Aligning the side (armhole) edges, sew the Bodice Front to the Bodice Back at the shoulders, stitch for stitch, using a mattress stitch (Glossary, page 138). The remaining stitches along the center back neck will correspond to the number of stitches listed for Back Neck Width Without Edging (39 in Mary's case). To determine the desired armhole depth, hang the joined sweater bodice from your shoulders, allowing the shoulder seams to drape naturally along the tops of your arms. (At this point don't worry about aligning the shoulder seams with the exact tops of your shoulders; you'll do that later.) Grasp the sides of the front and back under your arm where you'd like the base of the armhole to be—allow between 2¹/₂" and 3" of ease under your arm for a classic loose-fitting women's sweater (less for children, more for men). Pin the front and back together at this point, aligning the pin with a single row of knitting on each side.

Lay the bodice on a flat surface so that the wrong sides of the front and back face together and the pinned side edges are aligned. Measure straight down from the fold (which should be near, but may not be exactly at the shoulder seam) to the horizontal pin marking the base of the armhole. Enter this measurement in the Fitter List for Armhole Depth (Mary used a depth of 9¹/₂"). Double this number for the upper arm circumference and enter this number in the Fitter List for Upper Arm Circumference (Mary used a circumference of 19").

Remove the pins, carefully refold the bodice pieces exactly at the shoulder seam, and use safety pins to pin the side seams from the lower edges to the desired armhole depth. Try on the bodice again to confirm that you're happy with the armhole depth (if not, make any necessary adjustments and note them on the Fitter List).

Sleeve Length

Allowing the bodice to drape off your shoulders, ask a friend to measure along the top of your arm from the edge of the bodice shoulder seam down your bent arm to the desired sleeve length (including edging). Enter this in the Fitter List for Sleeve Length With Edging. Decide how much of the total sleeve length you want to be in the edging pattern and enter this number in the Fitter List for Cuff Length (Mary allowed for ¹/₂"). Subtract the cuff length from the total sleeve length and enter this number in the Fitter List for Sleeve Length Without Edging. This is the length over which the sleeve taper will take place.

About Decreases

In most knitting methods (including the English and Continental), the k2tog decrease slants to the right and the ssk decrease slants to the left (Glossary, page 135). Sometimes it doesn't matter which way the decrease slants—all that matters is that you reduce the number of stitches in the row. But sometimes when you're shaping a neckline, you'll want the decreases on each side of the opening to slant toward each other or in opposite directions.

The directions for k2tog and ssk can be misleading to some knitters—I'm one of them. I knit the Eastern crossed method, which means that my stitches appear twisted on the needle compared to those who use the more common English or Continental methods of knitting. My ssk is the same as someone else's k2tog. I avoid the confusion by thinking of the direction of slant of the decrease rather than the name: a right decrease slants to the right, a left decrease slants to the left. No matter how you knit, this will make sense.

Working increases and decreases in the first and last 2 stitches of a row together leaves knot-like bumps in the selvedge edge. These bumps make it difficult to sew a smooth seam. Indenting increases or decreases by working them one stitch in from the selvedge edge makes the selvedge appear regular, thereby making it easier to sew a flawless seam.

Measuring sleeve length this way allows you to take the drape of the knitting into consideration. Drape can vary widely from one fabric to the next, so it's always wise to adjust your sleeve length every time you knit in a new fabric, even if you follow the same pattern. Length can be added or subtracted at the cuff or shoulder end of the sleeve, so you don't have to recalculate the sleeve taper.

Cuff Circumference

With a measuring tape, measure the circumference of your wrist (or arm) at the point where you want the cuff to fall. Be sure to take into account the way you want the cuff to fit, i.e., loose or snug. Enter this number in the Fitter List for Cuff Circumference. Mary used a cuff circumference of $7^1/_2$". Divide this number by two for the Half Cuff Circumference ($3^3/_4$" for Mary's sweater).

8 Determine Sleeve Taper

Now that you know the dimensions of your sleeve, you can figure out exactly how to shape the taper from the cuff to the shoulder (or vice versa). And you can use the bodice that you've already knitted to determine the exact numbers of rows and stitches involved.

Tip **Determining Armhole Depth**

With a drop-shoulder sweater, the armhole should be deep enough to provide plenty of ease at the shoulders. Because this type of sweater has no armhole or sleeve cap shaping, the armhole depth is equal to half the width of the top of the sleeve.

If the armhole is too shallow, the sleeve will be too tight and will cause the neckline to pull towards the armholes and the sleeves to bind under the arms

If the armhole is too deep, the sleeves may have excess fabric that bunches under the arms. (Note that a kimono style has a drop shoulder with a deep armhole and a straight or nearly straight sleeve. This style lends itself very elegantly to a lightweight or drapey fabric, but can be cumbersome knitted in a standard worsted fabric.)

First, lay the bodice on a flat surface. If the surface is slippery, place a large towel between it and the bodice. Or pin the bodice to a blocking board. Position the bodice so that the selvedges are oriented at the top and bottom and the cast-on and bind-off rows are at the right and left—the rows of knitting will be oriented vertically. Take care to set up the fabric correctly and make sure that it doesn't bias or torque. (You may want to steam-press the fabric lightly to even out the stitches first.) Use a yardstick or other nonflexible straightedge (not a measuring tape) to take measurements, and be sure to measure along a straight line (or "ladder") of stitches or rows.

Sleeve Length

Using a yardstick, measure the length you entered on the Fitter List for Sleeve Length Without Edging, being careful to follow along a line (ladder) of stitches. Be sure to measure in the center of the fabric, away from the cast-on or bind-off rows, or any edgings that may affect stitch gauge. Mark the stitches at each end of the desired length with crossed pins. We'll call these Point A and Point B on the illustration on page 25. Count the number of rows between these points (130 rows for Mary's sweater). Round it off to an even number and enter this number in the Fitter List for the number of rows in Sleeve Length Without Edging.

Armhole Depth

Place the "0" end of the yardstick at Point A and orient it vertically so that it follows a single row of knitting. Measure the length you entered on the Fitter List for Armhole Depth ($9^1/_2$" for Mary's sweater), and mark this point with crossed pins. We'll call this Point C. Count the number of stitches between Point A and Point C and enter this number in the Fitter List for the number of stitches in Half Upper Arm Circumference (43 stitches for Mary's sweater).

Half Cuff Circumference

Place the "0" end of the yardstick at Point B and orient it vertically so that it follows a single row of knitting. Measure the length you entered on the Fitter List for Half Cuff Circumference, and mark this point with crossed pins. We'll call this Point D. Count the number of stitches between Point B and Point D and enter this number in the Fitter List for the number of stitches in Half Cuff Circumference (3¾" for Mary's sweater). Double this number and enter it for the number of stitches in Cuff Circumference.

Determine Sleeve Taper

Now that you know the numbers of stitches and rows in the sleeve, you can draw it to scale on graph paper, allowing each square to represent 1 stitch, and plot the exact taper as shown on page 27. You can use any type of graph paper, but only knitter's proportional graph paper will show the correct shape of the sleeve. You need to plot only the front (or back) half of the sleeve.

Using the numbers of stitches and rows entered in the Fitter List and allowing 1 square of graph paper to represent 1 stitch, draw a horizontal line for Sleeve Length Without Edging, and label Point A and Point B as before. Draw a vertical line down from Point A for the Half Upper Arm Circumference, and label the base of the line Point C. Draw another vertical line down from Point B for the Half Cuff Circumference, and label the base of this line Point D.

Place a ruler between Point C and Point D and draw a straight line to connect the two. This line represents the seam line of the sleeve and shows the number of stitches that will have to be increased if you knit upward from the cuff or the number of stitches that will have to be decreased if you knit downward from the shoulder. Starting at Point C, follow along to Point D and use a pencil to mark a dot at every point where this line crosses a horizontal line of the graph paper. Every dot represents a stitch that will need to be increased (if you're working

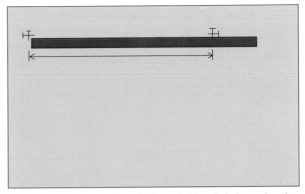

Measure the desired sleeve length along a ladder of stitches and mark the boundaries with crossed pins. Count the number of rows between these points.

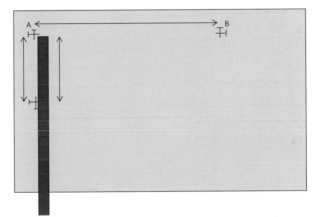

Lay a yardstick along the row line at point A and mark the desired armhole depth with crossed pins. Count the number of stitches between these points.

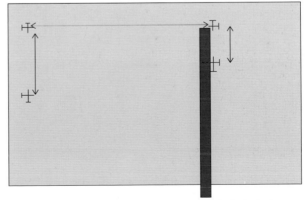

Lay a yardstick along the row line at point B and mark the desired armhole depth with crossed pins. Count the number of stitches between crossed pin markers.

upward from the cuff) or decreased (if you're working downward from the shoulder). Keep in mind that because only half of the sleeve is plotted, each dot represents a total of 2 stitches increased or decreased—1 stitch at each end of the needle. Now count the number of vertical lines in the graph paper (representing rows) between the dots to determine the number of rows between increases (or decreases). For example, if your dots appear every 4 rows, you'll want to work the increases (or decreases) at the beginning and end of every 4th row.

Most likely, there won't be a consistent number of rows between dots. For example, there might be 3 rows between some dots and 4 rows between others. In this case, you'll need to alternate between working 3 and 4 rows between the shaping rows. If the number of rows between dots involves fractions, as in 4½ rows between dots, you'll want to alternate between 5 rows and 4 rows between shaping rows. As long as you finish with the desired number of stitches and rows, and as long as you've maintained a relatively consistent rate of increases or decreases, the sleeve will end up the right size and shape. Some knitters prefer to work shaping on right-side rows only. If they are faced with a taper rate that involves an odd number of rows, say 5, which would call for every other shaping row to be a wrong-side row, they'll adjust the rate so that the shaping is worked on right-side rows. This was the case for Mary's sleeve. So that she could work her decreases (she worked downward from the shoulder) on right-side rows only, she simply alternated working the decreases on the 6th row, then the 4th.

9 Knit the Sleeves

The first step is to decide whether you want to knit the sleeves from cuff to shoulder or shoulder to cuff. It doesn't matter which you choose. For drop-shoulder sweaters, I prefer to pick up and knit stitches around the armhole and knit downward to the cuff, eliminating the need to

sew the sleeve into the armhole. I also like that the pick-up edge has less bulk than a sewn seam, and that I can try on the sweater to ensure that I like the length before I bind off the stitches. For bulky sweaters, though, I might choose to knit the sleeves upward from the cuffs so that I can work them in individual pieces, rather than having them attached to the bodice. Also, if I plan to include a special edging or ribbing on the cuff, I'll choose to work the sleeve from the cuff upward. But either way, the taper rate will be the same, because the cuff is not included in the taper rate calculation.

Cast On or Pick Up Sleeve Stitches

If you want to work your sleeve from the cuff to the shoulder, you'll cast on the number of stitches entered in the Fitter List for Cuff Circumference. If you want to work downward from the shoulder, you'll begin with the number of stitches entered for Upper Arm Circumference. If you want to work the sleeve seperately, simply cast on this number of stitches. If you want to pick up stitches for the upper arm around the armhole, you'll want to make sure that those stitches are evenly spaced all the way around the front and back armhole. To do so, lay the bodice on a flat surface with the right side of the knitting facing upward. Place a straight pin at the shoulder seam line to mark the center of the sleeve. Place an additional pin each on the front and back at the desired armhole depth (according to the number of rows for Armhole Depth in the Fitter List). For Mary's sweater, she placed pins 9½" down from the shoulder (66 rows). Divide the number of stitches entered for Upper Arm Circumference by two to determine the number of stitches to pick up and knit from each the front and back. Mary had an Upper Arm Circumference of 86 stitches, so she picked up 43 stitches each along the front and back armhole.

With the right side facing and beginning at the base of the armhole, pick up and knit (Glossary, page 135) the designated number of stitches between pins, removing the pins as you come to them.

10 Join Seams

Using the seaming method of your choice (Glossary, page 136), sew the pieces together. If you picked up stitches for the sleeves, you'll only have to sew the sleeve and side seams. If you knitted the sleeves separately, you'll need to sew the upper sleeve to the bodice front and back (centered on the shoulder seam) before sewing the sleeve and side seams.

11 Add Edgings

Now it's time to add edgings. To finish the neckline, you'll want to pick up and knit stitches around the neck opening and work a few rows of a noncurling edging pattern (Mary used knit 1, purl 1 rib). With double-pointed needles or a short (16") circular needle, pick up and knit stitches evenly spaced around the neckline opening. The number of stitches to pick up depends on the size of the opening and your stitch gauge. In general, pick up 1 stitch for every stitch along a bind-off edge (i.e., along the back neck and lower front neck), and pick up about 3 stitches for every 4 rows along sloped edges (i.e., along the angled edges of the front neck) for an edging that lies flat. Join for working in rounds and work your choice of edgings for the desired number of rounds (Mary worked 4 rounds). Loosely bind off the stitches following the pattern stitch (i.e., knit 1, purl 1 rib) with one size larger needle.

> **Tip Armhole Depth Measurements**
> To make sure that you have measured to the same point on the front and back, count the number of selvedge stitches along the side seam line. Not only will this help you pick up stitches evenly along the front and back armhole, it will also ensure that there will be the same number of stitches between the armhole and hem on the front and back and that the side seams will be even without puckers.

12 Finishing Touches

Work in loose ends with a tapestry needle. Steam-press or block the sweater.

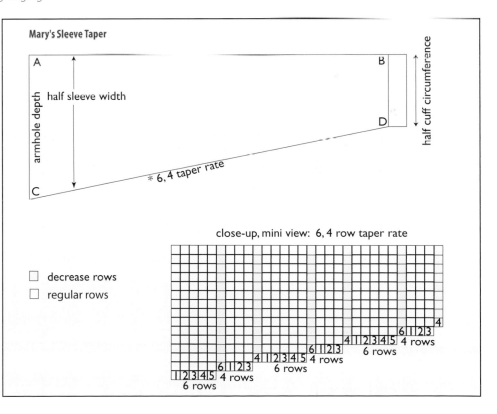

Mary's Sleeve Taper

armhole depth · half sleeve width · half cuff circumference

A · B · C · D

* 6, 4 taper rate

□ decrease rows
□ regular rows

close-up, mini view: 6, 4 row taper rate

4
6 1 2 3 · 4 rows
4 1 2 3 4 5 · 4 rows · 6 rows
6 1 2 3 · 6 rows
4 1 2 3 4 5 · 4 rows · 6 rows
6 1 2 3 · 6 rows
1 2 3 4 5 · 4 rows
6 rows

Chapter Four

Side-to-Side Construction

Sweaters that are knitted from side to side are worked parallel to the center line of the body. This method creates slimming vertical rows of stitches that are especially prominent when worked in garter stitch or color stripes. Although the difference in construction between up-and-down and side-to-side knitting is straightforward, the two fabrics will handle differently. To ensure that a fabric knitted side to side won't stretch too much in length, knit a generous swatch. Stretch the swatch both widthwise and lengthwise. Choose a yarn and stitch pattern that stretches minimally in width, or be prepared to make adjustments to your pattern to make up for that stretch. For our example, Mary knitted her classic crew from side to side.

The Fitter List for Drop-Shoulder Sweater Knitted Side to Side

Measure your body and allow for the appropriate amount of ease (see page 14) or measure a sweater that fits the way you like and enter the numbers below. Refer to your gauge swatch for your stitch and row gauges, then translate each measurement into numbers of stitches and/or rows as you go along.

Yarn

Yarn name: __Ashland Bay Trader's Falkland Superwash__

Fiber content: __Superwash wool handdyed by Lynne Vogel__

Weight classification: __Worsted (#4 Medium)__

WPI: __11__

Number of yards/pounds used: __1,180 yards; 15½ ounces__

Gauge

Stitches per inch: __4½__ Rows per inch: __7__ Needle size: __US 8 (5 mm)__

Details

Cast-on method: __Provisional__

Bind-off method: __Chain__

Selvedge treatment: __Chain stitch__

Sleeve increase/decrease method: __Paired decreases__

Seam technique: __Mattress stitch__

Notes/Variations

Mary wanted to make the decreases on right-side rows only, so she used a taper of *6, 4. The first set of paired decreases was made on the 6th row, the next pair of decreases was made 4 rows after that; the 6, 4 sequence was repeated from * 12 more times to complete the total number of decreases.

Sweater Measurements

Bodice

Circumference: __45__ inches

Width: __22½__ inches; __160__ rows

Cast-On Stitches: __103__ stitches

Length With Edging: __23__ inches

Length Without Edging: __22½__ inches; __101__ stitches

Length of Lower Edging: __½__ inches; __4__ rows

Armhole Depth: __9½__ inches; __42__ stitches

Back Neck Width Without Edging: __8½__ inches; __60__ rows

Back Neck Width With Edging: __7__ inches

Front Neck Depth Without Edging: __2½__ inches; __12__ stitches

Front Neck Depth With Edging: __1½__ inches

Lower Front Neck Width: __6½__ inches; __46__ rows

Begin Front Neck At: __6½__ inches; __50__ rows

Shoulder Width: __7__ inches; __50__ rows

Sleeves

Sleeve Length Without Edging: __18½__ inches; __130__ rows

Sleeve Length With Edging: __19__ inches; __134__ rows

Cuff Circumference: __7½__ inches; __34__ stitches

Half Cuff Circumference: __3¾__ inches; __17__ stitches

Cuff Length: __½__ inches; __4__ rows

Upper Arm Circumference: __19__ inches; __86__ stitches

Half Upper Arm Circumference: __9½__ inches; __43__ stitches

Sleeve Taper Rate: __2__ stitches decreased every __5__ rows __26__ times; __130__ rows

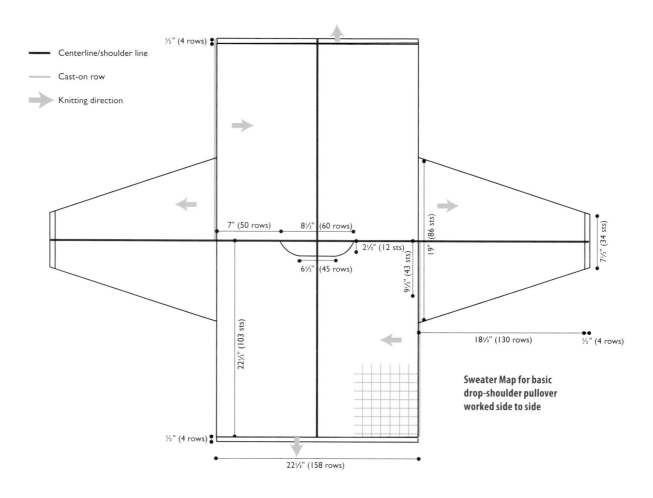

½" (4 rows)

— Centerline/shoulder line

— Cast-on row

→ Knitting direction

7" (50 rows)   8½" (60 rows)

2½" (12 sts)

6½" (45 rows)

9½" (43 sts)

19" (86 sts)

7½" (34 sts)

22½" (103 sts)

18½" (130 rows)   ½" (4 rows)

½" (4 rows)

**Sweater Map for basic
drop-shoulder pullover
worked side to side**

22½" (158 rows)

In side-to-side knitting, the cast-on and bind-off rows fall along the side seams (selvedge stitches fall along the side seams of up-and-down knitting). Because cast-on and bind-off edges typically have less stretch than a row of knitting, I recommend using a provisional cast-on method (Glossary, page 134) that stretches more like a regular row of knitting and allows me to finish the seam with a three-needle bind-off (Glossary, page 139). I also like to work matching cast-on and bind-off methods (see pages 131–134) so that both edges of the side seams look and feel the same. Selvedge stitches fall along the shoulder, neckline, and hemline of sweaters worked in this orientation.

1 Determine Gauge

Work as for the Up-and-Down Classic Crew (page 17).

2 Determine Bodice Circumference and Length

Work as for Up-and-Down Classic Crew (page 17).

3 Determine Stitch Count

Multiply your stitch gauge by your desired bodice length (minus edging) to determine the number of stitches you'll need to get that length. Mary had a gauge of 4½ stitches per inch and wanted a length of 22½" (before edging). She therefore needed 101 stitches (4.5 stitches per inch x 22.5 inches = 101.25 stitches). Round this number down to 101 and enter this number of stitches in the Fitter List for Bodice Length Without Edging.

Now's the time to decide if you want to add selvedge stitches (see page 18) to facilitate seaming later. Add the selvedge stitches to the stitches in Bodice Length Without Edging to get the Cast On Stitches. Mary wanted to use a chain selvedge and sew the seams with a mattress stitch 1 stitch from the selvedge edge at the shoulders and she wanted to pick up and knit stitches 1 stitch from the edge of the other selvedge for the lower edging. This meant she'd lose the equivalent of 2 stitches total in the length, which translates to almost ½" in the total finished length. To make up for this difference, Mary chose to add an extra stitch at each selvedge edge, so she increased her cast-on number to 103 stitches.

To determine the number of rows you'll need to work a side-to-side garment to get the desired bodice width, multiply your row gauge by the desired bodice width. Enter this number in the Fitter List for the number of rows in Bodice Width.

> ## Tip Smooth Side Seams
> To help ensure smooth side seams that have the same amount of stretch as a row of knitting, use a provisional cast-on and three-needle bind-off (or Kitchener stitch grafting) for sweaters knitted side to side.

4 Knit the Bodice Back

Using the method of your choice (Glossary, page 132–134) cast on the desired number of stitches for Bodice Length. Mary used the provisional cast-on. Work your chosen pattern (Mary used stockinette stitch) until the piece measures about 3" from the cast-on row. Lay the piece on a flat surface and measure the width of the row to confirm that it corresponds to the desired Body Length Without Edging. (To get an accurate measurement here, slip the stitches onto a long circular needle or onto waste yarn while you measure, then return them to the working needles.) If the piece is not the correct size, remeasure your gauge on this piece of fabric, recalculate the number of stitches to cast on according to your desired measurement, and reknit the piece to this point. Once you're satisfied that the width of the row is correct, continue in your chosen stitch pattern until the piece measures the desired Bodice Width (Mary knitted for 160 rows). Leave the stitches live by running waste yarn through them.

Measure the Bodice Width and count the final number of rows. Enter those numbers in the Fitter List for Bodice Width.

The Bodice Back is the desired width, but the ribbing (or other edging) needs to be added to the lower edge before it's the desired length. You'll do this by picking up and knitting (Glossary, page 135) stitches along one selvedge edge and working these stitches in the desired stitch pattern for the desired length (Mary worked knit 1, purl 1 rib for ½").

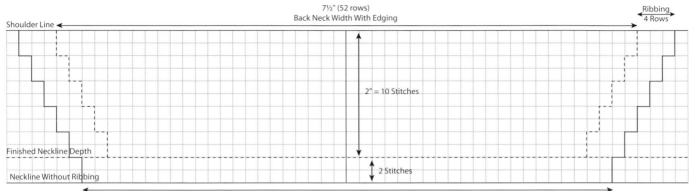

Neckline Graph. Each square of the neckline chart represents 1 stitch. The neck edge is shaped by decreasing stitches along one side of the neck, working straight for the desired distance, then increasing stitches to shape the other side.

5 Determine Front Neckline Width and Depth

You'll use the knitted Bodice Back to map out the exact number of stitches and rows involved in the neck opening on the Bodice Front. First, find the centerline of the knitted Bodice Back. If you worked an even number of rows, the centerline will be the boundary between 2 rows—mark this line with a vertical pin. If you worked an odd number of rows, the center line will be an entire row—place a vertical pin on each side of the center row.

Standing in front of a mirror, hold the Bodice Back against your body, aligning the centerline of the bodice with the centerline of your body. Pin the shoulder edges of the Bodice Back (without stretching or pulling the piece) to the shoulder lines of the shirt you're wearing, leaving the center part unpinned to suggest the desired neck width. This will give you a good idea of how the finished sweater will hang. Mark the desired finished neck width and depth just as for the Up-and-Down Classic Crew (page 20).

Remove the Bodice Back from your shirt and lay it on a flat surface. With a ruler or tape measure, measure the neck width between the vertical pins and enter this number in the Fitter List for Back Neck Width With Edging. Count the number of rows between the pins and enter this number as well. Measure the neck depth from the shoulder line to the marking pin and enter this number for Front Neck Depth With Edging. Count the number of stitches between the shoulder line and marking pin, round up or down to achieve an even number, and enter this number as well.

Chart the Neckline on Graph Paper

Once you know how wide and deep you want your neckline in terms of rows and stitches, you can detail the exact shape on graph paper, allowing each square of the graph paper to represent 1 stitch. If possible, use knitter's proportional graph paper (Resources, page 142) so the shape you draw will match the shape you'll knit, but be sure to turn the graph paper on its side to represent side-to-side knitting.

First, draw a horizontal line to represent the shoulder line. Bisect this with a vertical line to represent the center front. If you worked an even number of rows for the bodice (as Mary did), draw the centerline on a vertical line of the graph paper to represent the boundary between 2 rows. If you worked an odd number of rows, shade in a vertical column of squares to represent the center front row. Draw a dashed horizontal line at the desired finished neckline depth. This represents the neckline after the ribbing has been added. Mary wanted a finished neckline depth of 2", which translates to 9 stitches at her gauge of 4.5 stitches to the inch. Mary rounded this up to 10 stitches to get an even number and account for her selvedge. Next, account for the depth of neckline ribbing by drawing another horizontal line the appropriate number of stitches below for the neckline depth without ribbing. Mary wanted 1/2" of ribbing, which translates to about 2 stitches. Mary's total neck depth (before ribbing) is therefore 12 stitches (10 stitches plus 2 stitches). Enter this number of rows in the Fitter List for Front Neck Depth Without Edging.

Next, mark the desired finished back neck width along the horizontal shoulder line, centered about the centerline. Mary wanted a Back Neck Width With Edging of 7 1/2", which at her gauge of 7 rows to the inch, translates to 52.5 rows. Mary rounded this down to an even 52 rows. To allow for the 1/2" neckband, Mary needed to allow 8 1/2" for the Back Neck Width Without Edging, which translates to 59.5 rows, which she rounded up to 60 rows. Mark the slope between the back and front neck by drawing lines from the edges of the back neck width (without ribbing) to the front neck depth (without ribbing). Draw these as jagged

> ### Tip Adding Stitch Patterns
> If you wish to knit this sweater with a repeating stitch pattern, you may need to adjust your cast-on number to accommodate full pattern repeats and to center the pattern.

lines, working down 2 boxes (stitches), then toward the center line 2 boxes (rows), until you reach the line marking the neck depth (without ribbing). These lines represent a 2-stitch bind-off for every 2 rows of knitting, which produces a nice rounded neck. Count the number of stitches that remain between the jagged lines on the neck depth (44 rows in Mary's case) and enter this number in the Fitter List for Lower Front Neck Width. Note that the width of the lower front neck is different from that calculated for the Up-and-Down Classic Crew (page 21). This is a result of the difference between the stitch and row gauge.

6 Knit the Bodice Front

Knit the Bodice Front just like the Bodice Back to where the neckline shaping begins. To determine where to begin the neckline, subtract the number of rows in Back Neck Width Without Edging (60 rows in Mary's case) from the number of rows in the Bodice Width (160 rows for Mary). The result is the total number of rows for the shoulders. For Mary, this was 100 rows. Divide this number by

> ### Tip Picking Up Stitches
> The number of stitches to pick up and knit depends on your gauge and stitch pattern. If you're picking up stitches along a stockinette-stitch fabric, pick up about 3 stitches for every 4 rows. If you're picking up stitches along a garter-stitch fabric, pick up 1 stitch for every 2 rows. You may have to adjust these ratios to achieve a smooth pick-up row that neither puckers nor gaps. Don't be afraid to rip out if you don't like how it looks. If you want a snug ribbing that draws in, knit it with needles one or two sizes smaller than used for the bodice.

two to get the number of rows for each shoulder (50 rows for Mary). Enter this number in the Fitter List for the rows in Begin Neckline Shaping as well as in Shoulder Width.

When you get to this point, shape the left neck edge by following the neckline graph, binding off 2 stitches at the beginning of every right-side row the appropriate number of times (6 times for Mary), then work even for the number of rows corresponding to the Lower Front Neck Width (44 rows for Mary), then shape the right neck edge by casting on 2 stitches every other row until you get back to the original number of stitches. Work even until you've worked the same number of rows as in the Bodice Back.

Add ribbing (or other edging) to the lower body (waist) edge as you did for the back.

Gently steam-block the pieces, unless you're working with a synthetic fiber such as nylon that doesn't require blocking.

7 Determine Sleeve Dimensions

Now you're ready to begin the sleeves. First, you'll need to measure the desired armhole depth, sleeve length from cuff to armhole, and cuff circumference. Although you can take these measurements on your body or from a sweater that fits the way you like, you'll get much better results if you take them with respect to the pieces you've already knitted.

Aligning the side (armhole) edges, sew the Bodice Front to the Bodice Back at the shoulders, row for row, using a mattress stitch seam. The remaining rows along the center back neck will correspond to the number of rows listed for Back Neck Width Without Edging (60 in Mary's case)

Determine the desired Armhole Depth, Sleeve Length, and Cuff Circumference as for the Up-and-Down Classic Crew (pages 23–24).

8 Determine Sleeve Taper

Work as for the Up-and-Down Classic Crew (page 24).

9 Knit the Sleeves

Work as for the Up-and-Down Classic Crew (page 26). If you plan to knit the sleeves from the shoulder down to the cuff, you'll pick up stitch for stitch—the first row of the sleeve will have the same number of stitches as are around the bodice armhole. (If you want, you can keep the armhole stitches live on the bodice back and front and simply continue working them for the sleeves.)

10 Join Seams

Using the method of your choice (Glossary, page 136) sew the pieces together (Mary used a mattress stitch) to join the sleeve seams. Join the side seams with a three-needle bind-off (Glossary, page 139). If you picked up stitches for the sleeves (or continued knitting bodice fabric to armhole depth to form sleeves), you'll only have to sew the sleeve and side seams. If you knitted the sleeves separately, you'll need to sew the upper sleeve to the bodice front and back (centered on the shoulder seam) before sewing the sleeve and side seams.

> *Tip* **Seamless Bodice**
> Join the side seams with the Kitchener stitch (Glossary, page 136) for a seamless bodice.

11 Add Edgings

To finish the neckline, you'll want to pick up and knit stitches around the neck opening and work a few rows of a noncurling edging pattern (Mary used knit 1, purl 1 rib). With double-pointed needles or a short (16") circular needle, pick up and knit stitches evenly spaced around the neckline opening. In general, pick up 1 stitch for every stitch along a bind-off or cast-on edge (i.e., along the angled edges of the front neck), and pick up about 3 stitches for every 4 rows along straight edges (i.e. along the back neck and front neck) for an edging that lies flat. Join for working in rounds and work your choice of edgings for the desired number of rounds (Mary worked 4 rounds). Loosely bind off the stitches following the pattern stitch (i.e., k1, p1 rib) with one size larger needle.

12 Finishing Touches

Work in loose ends with a tapestry needle. Steam-press or block the sweater.

Chapter Five

Variations

Now that you know the ins and outs of the Classic Crew pattern, you can make adjustments to fit your own individual style. Below are the variations we used in our sweaters (you'll find these mapped out in detail in the projects that follow). Armed with the Fitter List and Sweater Map, you'll find it easy to design your own variations.

Cardigan Option

The Classic Crew is shown as a pullover, but it's easy enough to transform it into a cardigan. Simply split the bodice along the center front and work the front in two pieces.

If you're working up and down, you'll knit the bodice front in two halves, each of which will have the armhole shaping along one selvedge edge and the neck shaping on the other. (Be sure to work the armhole and neck as mirror images for the second front so that you don't end up with two left fronts). The center front edge will be the selvedge edge of pieces worked up and down.

If you're working side to side, you can make the center front edges the cast-on edges and work outward to the side seams, or you can work in the opposite direction from the side seams to the center front, in which case, the center front edge is the bind-off edge.

Remember that if you make a cardigan, split the neck line graph between the two fronts, so that the centerline of the graph corresponds to the center front opening.

Whichever way you work, you'll want to finish the front edges. You can pick up and knit stitches along the center front edges and work side to side, as for Lori's Jacob's Windows Sweater (page 68), or the Rectangle Vest (page 75), Sandy's Cardigan for Zylie (page 87). Alternatively, you can work extra stitches (or rows, depending on whether you're working up and down or side to side) along with the bodice fronts, as for Alina's Basketweave Coat (page 53), or Laurie's Panel Jacket (page 112). Either way, plan for the placement of buttons before you work the buttonhole band (see Alina's Tip for Button Placement, page 59) so that you can incorporate buttonholes as you go.

Opposite: Jacob's Ladder Sweater, a cardigan variation.

Neck Variations

There are a number of ways to adjust the shape of the neck, from a straight boat neck to a V neck. And once you've shaped that neck, you can add a collar.

Turtleneck

It's easy to add more rows of edging to make the basic round neck into a turtleneck, as Linda did for her One-Piece Turtleneck (page 60). Linda worked the edging for 2¹/₂″, but you could make it as long as you like. If you like a firmer edging, work the neckline edging for twice the desired length and fold it under to the wrong side for a double thickness, as Gail did for her Red Aran (page 95).

Collar

If you want to add a collar as on Alina's Basketweave Coat (page 53), Sandy's Cardigan for Zylie (page 87), or Lori's Jacob's Windows (page 68) , you'll start by shaping the neckline according to the basic pattern. Then pick up and knit stitches (typically 1 stitch for every stitch or row) around the neckline and knit the collar outward.

If you want the collar to stand up Mandarin style, pick up and knit a stitch for every stitch and every row around the neckline opening, as Alina did for her Basketweave Coat, work the desired stitch pattern for the desired length, then bind off all the stitches to form the outer edge of the collar. If you want the collar to fold over and lie flat, as in Sandy's Sweater for Zylie and Lori's Jacob's Windows sweater, increase a stitch in every 4th stitch of the 2nd row and/or increase a stitch at each shoulder seam line every other row until the collar is the desired width.

Boat Neck

The boat neck is the simplest of necklines, nothing more than a horizontal slit at the shoulder line. You'll find it in the Bouclé Boat Neck (page 48) and Angel Wing Lace Float (page 104). Although the neck is unshaped, the flexible knitted fabric drapes into a soft curve on both of these sweaters. If you combine a boat neck with a cardigan, as in the Rectangle Vest (page 75), the upper edges of the fronts will fold over to make soft lapels.

To make a boat neck, all you have to do is decide how wide you want the neckline. Because there is no neckline shaping, there is no need to determine the depth of neckline opening, and no need to plot it on graph paper. Simply knit the bodice front identical to the bodice back and sew the shoulder seams for the desired width.

If you're working up and down, the neckline will be the bind-off edge (if you worked from the lower edge upwards) or the cast-on edge (if you worked from the neck

Neck Variations

One-Piece Turtleneck

Red Aran

Basketweave Coat

Cardigan for Zylie

downwards). If you're working side to side, the neckline will be the selvedge edge. Depending on how you treat the edges and the finished look you're after, you may or may not want to add a finished border.

V Neck

To change the Classic Crew into a V neck, as in the Rose-to-Blue Sweater (page 81), plot the neckline on graph paper as described, marking the desired back neckline width (without ribbing) along the shoulder line and the desired depth of the V along the centerline of the bodice. Draw diagonal lines to indicate the V shape from the base of the V to the back neck. Following the lines on the graph paper, draw the taper lines upwards from the base of the V to the shoulder line. Ideally, the taper should be an even sequence; for example, decrease 1 stitch every 2 rows or decrease 1 stitch every 4 rows. If the taper calls to decrease 1 stitch after 3 rows, then after 4 rows, then after 3 rows, etc., and you don't want to work the uneven sequence, simply adjust the width of the back neckline until the slope fits a more uniform sequence. Or decrease at an even rate until you reach the desired back neckline width, then continue even on those stitches to the shoulder line.

Remember that the measurements for the V neck, before adding the border, should be deeper and wider in order to accommodate the border and create the final

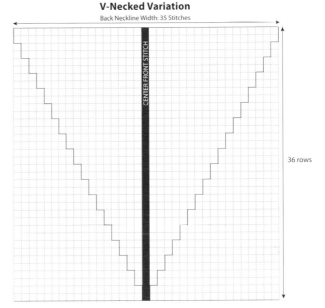

V-Necked Variation
Back Neckline Width: 35 Stitches

CENTER FRONT STITCH

36 rows

Plot the V neckline on graph paper, tapering it to the desired depth.

neckline size you want.

If you're working a V neck up and down, work the front in two halves from the base of the V to the shoulders. Shape the neckline taper by working right-leaning decreases (Glossary page 135) on one side and left-leaning decreases on the other. It doesn't matter which type of decrease you work on which half as long as you're consistent.

If you're working from side to side, you'll shape the neckline by binding off stitches to shape the first half of the V, then casting on stitches to shape the second half.

Jacob's Windows

Bouclé Boatneck

Angel Wing Lace Float

Rectangle Vest

Rose-to-Blue V Neck

Shoulder Variations

The Classic Crew has drop-shoulder shaping at the armhole, which is the easiest to knit because it involves a straight edge with no shaping. This type of armhole hangs off the shoulder so that the seam between the sleeve and bodice falls somewhere along the upper arm. There are a number of other ways to work the shoulder of a sweater and, of course, the Twisted Sisters tried a few.

Modified Drop Shoulder

If you want the armhole seam to fall closer to your actual shoulder line, you can modify the drop shoulder by making the bodice narrower along the length of the armhole and making the sleeve longer to fill the resulting gap. The extra length on the sleeve can be shaped with a notch or an angle. The way that the notch or angle is shaped depends on whether you're working up and down or side to side. I worked a notched armhole side to side in the Rectangle Vest (page 75); Alina worked an angle armhole up and down in her Basketweave Coat (page 53).

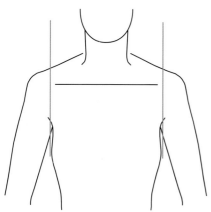

Measure across your upper chest from armpit to armpit to determine your "across-front" measurement.

Shape the Armhole: The first step is to decide where you want the vertical armhole seams to be. If you're working up and down, knit the bodice back to the desired armhole depth and pin the bodice to your shoulders as for the Classic Crew. Mark your desired across-front measurement centered along the centerline. Then simply count the number of stitches outside the desired front measurement—this is the number of stitches

Shoulder Variations

The bodice on a modified drop-shoulder sweater is narrower than on a drop-shoulder sweater, and the sleeves extend into the armholes along a notch or angle.

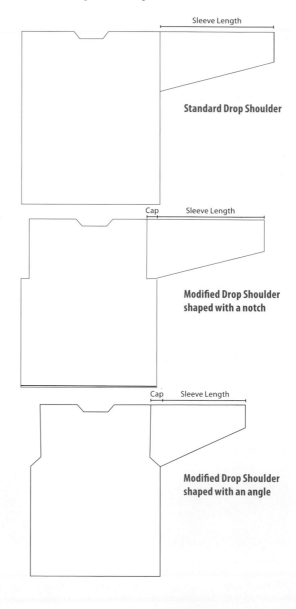

Sleeve Length

Standard Drop Shoulder

Cap   Sleeve Length

Modified Drop Shoulder shaped with a notch

Cap   Sleeve Length

Modified Drop Shoulder shaped with an angle

to bind off at each armhole. To shape the armhole with a notch, bind off the specified number of stitches at the base of the armhole and work the remainder of the bodice even to the shoulders. To shape the armhole with an angle, bind off 1 stitch at the base of the armhole, then decrease 1 stitch at the armhole edge every other row until you have removed the specified number of stitches. Then work the remainder of the bodice even to the shoulders.

If you're working your sweater side to side, you'll be removing rows instead of stitches. If you're working from the centerline of the bodice to the side seam, you'll work the bodice to the shoulder line, then bind off the number of stitches that corresponds to the armhole depth, and continue even on the remaining stitches until the lower bodice is the desired width to the side seam. If you're working from side seam to side seam, begin by subtracting the number of stitches that corresponds to the total armhole depth from the total number of stitches to cast on, work the desired width to the shoulder line, then cast on the number of stitches that corresponds to the armhole depth.

To shape a notched armhole, work underarm cast-ons or bind-offs (depending on the direction you're working) all at once. To work an angled armhole, spread out the underarm cast-ons and bind-offs over several rows by increasing (or decreasing) 1 stitch every other row the desired number of times.

Shape the Sleeve: To make a sleeve that matches the modified armhole, you'll need to figure the sleeve taper on the underarm sleeve length instead of the length along the top of the sleeve. To find the underarm sleeve length of a modified drop-shoulder sweater, subtract the height of the sleeve cap, which has the same measurement as the width of armhole shaping from the over-arm sleeve length.

You'll also need to add rows to make up for the rows or stitches eliminated from the bodice. If the armhole has a notched shape, simply work the cap for the number of rows that corresponds to the width of the notch. If the armhole has an angled shape and you're working the sleeve upward from the wrist, shape the cap by binding off 1 stitch, then decreasing 1 stitch at each edge of the sleeve every other row to mirror the stitches decreased in the bodice. If you're working downward from the shoulder, begin with the number of stitches that corresponds to the straight part of the armhole, and shape the cap by increasing 1 stitch at each edge of the sleeve every other row to the armhole.

Shoulder Variations

Rectangle Vest

Basketweave Coat

Red Aran

Cardigan for Zylie

Saddle Shoulders

Another way to alter the shoulder is to work a horizontal strip that extends from the top of the sleeve along the top of the shoulder to the neck, as in Gail's Red Aran (page 95). Gail used this variation to allow her to place a continuous cable motif from the neck to the sleeve cuff.

Because the saddle falls along the shoulder line, it takes up area that otherwise is taken up by the Bodice Front and Bodice Back. Therefore, you'll want to shorten the armhole depth on one-half of the total saddle width. For example, if you want a 3"-wide saddle across the top of your shoulder and you want a 9" armhole, you'll want to knit the armhole on the bodice front and back to 7$^1/_2$". The remaining 1$^1/_2$" of armhole depth on each piece will be contributed by the saddle.

If you work the sleeve from shoulder to cuff, you'll start by casting on the appropriate number of stitches for the saddle width, knitting the saddle for the length of the shoulder, then casting on stitches (equally divided on each side of the saddle) to get the desired upper arm circumference. If you work the sleeve from cuff to shoulder, you'll work the sleeve as for the basic sweater up to the bind-off row. Rather than binding off all of the stitches, you'll just bind off the stitches on each side, leaving the appropriate number of stitches in the center to accommodate the saddle width, and working these center stitches for the length of the shoulder before binding them off.

Sandy knitted a saddle up and down on a side-to-side sweater in her Cardigan for Zylie (page 87). She wanted to deepen the armhole as an afterthought and liked the design element of garter ridges on the saddle. She picked up and knitted stitches along the shoulder bind-offs of the front bodice, knitted them in garter stitch for 1$^1/_4$", then sewed them to the back shoulders.

Shaped Shoulders

The Classic Crew has straight seams at the shoulders, formed by binding off (or casting on) stitches for the entire width of the shoulder at once. If you'd prefer to have the shoulders of your sweater more closely match the gentle slope from your shoulder to your neck, work the sweater up and down from the bottom up so that the shoulder line is the bind-off edge, and work the bind-off in a few steps, as Lori did in her Jacob's Windows sweater (page 68).

Divide the number of stitches to be bound off for each shoulder into thirds. Instead of binding off all of the stitches on a single row, bind off a third of them every other row, beginning at the armhole edge and progressing to the neck edge. If the number of shoulder stitches isn't evenly divisible by three, bind off the extra stitches in the first and second steps. For example, if you have 29 shoulder stitches, you'd bind off 10 stitches in the first group, 10 stitches in the second group, and 9 stitches in the final group.

Sleeve Variations

There are a number of ways to alter the sleeves of the Classic Crew. Some of them are not noticeable in the finished look of the sweater, but may facilitate knitting or seaming. Others make a difference in the overall appearance of the sweater.

Sleeves Worked as Continuation of Bodice

You can eliminate the need to sew sleeves into armholes by working the sleeves as extensions of the bodice stitches, as in Linda's One-Piece Turtleneck (page 60). Linda began by casting on stitches for the hem edge of the bodice back, then she worked upward to the armholes, cast on stitches at each end of the bodice for the length of the sleeves, and worked the sleeves in one piece with the upper part of the bodice, tapering her sleeves with short-rows. At the shoulder line, she reversed the process, and worked down to the hem edge of the bodice front (shaping the neck along the way). In the end, the only seams to sew were along the sides, from the lower bodice edge to the sleeve cuffs. There are no seams between the sleeves and bodice.

If you work a sweater side to side, you can begin by casting on stitches for a sleeve cuff, work the sleeve to the armhole, then cast on stitches at each edge of the upper sleeve for the bodice front and back, work across the bodice, adding the neckline as you go, then bind off all but the upper sleeve stitches, and work the sleeve downward to the cuff. The cast-on edge is at one cuff; the bind-off edge is at the other. To make the cast-on and bind-off edges look the same, use matching methods (see Glossary, pages 131–134).

Sleeves Knitted in the Round

If you prefer not to sew a sleeve seam, sleeves worked up and down can be worked in the round instead of back and forth, as in Lori's Jacob's Windows sweater (page 68). Using a short circular needle or a set of double-pointed needles, cast on the desired number of stitches, place a marker on the needle to denote the "seam" line, and join the stitches for working in rounds. You do not need to add selvedge stitches because there will be no seam. To shape the sleeve taper, work the necessary increases (if working cuff to shoulder) or decreases (if working shoulder to cuff) on each side of the marker. It looks best if you work a few stitches plain between the increases or decreases.

Adjusted Sleeve Length

It's easy to change the length of the sleeve on the basic sweater. For example, if you'd prefer three-quarter-length sleeves (as in the Angel Wing Lace Float on page 104), simply substitute the circumference of your forearm where you want the sleeve to end for your cuff circumference on the Fitter List, then plot the sleeve taper on graph paper as for the basic sweater, using the desired length for sleeve length without ribbing.

Adjusted Sleeve Shape

The basic sweater has traditional drop-shoulder shaping with sleeves that taper at a regular rate from the wide armhole to the narrow cuff. But you don't have to limit yourself to this shape. You can make sleeves that flare into bells by tapering as usual between the shoulder

Sleeve Variations

One-Piece Turtleneck

Angel Wing Lace Float

and three-quarter-length measurement, then increasing from there to the desired final length. The larger your cuff circumference, the more the sleeve will ruffle. It's also possible to flare the sleeve in a lacy fashion by stair-stepping needle sizes, working with progressively larger needles toward the cuff.

You can also get a drastically different look by extending the armhole all the way to the lower body edge, as in the Angel Wing Lace Float. For changes this major, it's a good idea to plot the pieces on proportional graph paper to make sure you'll end up with the shape you want. Or better yet, make a full-size template on Pellon pattern paper (see page 46). Shape the sleeve as you knit by periodically laying it directly on the template and working increases or decreases as necessary to duplicate that shape. Keep in mind that there will be a lot of stitches at the armhole edge and you'll want to use a long circular needle to accommodate them all.

If you're working up and down from the lower edge, you'd begin by casting on the appropriate number of stitches for the bodice width then increasing a stitch (or casting on a group of stitches) at each end of the needle every 2 rows or so to get the shape you want. If you're working side to side from the center of the bodice, you'd begin by casting on stitches for the bodice length, then decreasing stitches (or binding off a group of stitches) every 2 rows or so until you have the desired cuff width. If you're working in the opposite direction—from cuff to center—you'd begin with the appropriate number of cuff stitches, then work increases and cast-ons to achieve the total bodice length.

Edgings

Edgings around hems, cuffs, necklines, and front bands are a great way to add a little variation to the basic sweater. Decorative borders such as ribbing, lace, or even a band of garter or seed stitch will stabilize and prevent curling of the lower edges of hems and cuffs and give a finished look to neckbands, front bands, and collars. Edgings may be knitted as a part of the fabric (like a ribbed band along the hem or cuff) or they may be added later (like a collar or front band). Either way, they are an integral part of the overall look and should be considered at the outset.

Traditional sweaters have ribbing at the lower body, cuffs, and neck. Ribbing stabilizes the fabric so that it doesn't roll and snugs the fabric down to a narrower, more elastic, body-hugging fabric. But seed stitch and garter stitch also make attractive noncurling edges. And don't overlook the possibility of edgings that make bold statements, such as the ruffles (by increasing lots of stitches in a few rows) on the cuffs and neck of Crystal's Wild Thing (page 129).

Edging as Part of the Fabric

Ribbing and other stabilizing stitches are often knitted as a part of the sweater fabric, especially in the bodice and cuff. Including an edging in an up-and-down bodice is easy—simply cast on for the desired bodice width, knit the edging to your desired length, then knit the rest of the bodice in your desired stitch pattern, as in the up-down version of Mary's Classic Crew (page 15) and Lori's Jacob's Window Sweater (page 68).

On a side-to-side bodice, you can work a number of the stitches (usually 1" to 3" worth) at one selvedge edge in the desired noncurling pattern, as in the Rectangle Vest (page 75). In this orientation, the ridges in garter stitch will mimic the ribs in ribbing worked up and down. Or use seed stitch, which will look the same whether worked up and down or side to side. Remember that different stitch patterns may have different gauges, so you may need to add or subtract a few stitches to get the width you want.

In sweaters with boat-neck shaping, a noncurling stitch can be worked for the few stitches closest to the neckline, as in the Rectangle Vest (page 75). Similarly, a few stitches (if the bodice is worked up and down) or rows (if the bodice is worked side to side) can be worked in the edging pattern round the armholes of a vest. When these garments come off the needles, there's no need to finish the edges in any other way.

If you're working a sweater up and down from the neck to the hem, begin by working the edging pattern for the desired length of the neckband, then change to the desired stitch pattern for the rest of the body, as Gail did for her Red Aran (page 95).

If you work an edging for a sleeve cuff, be sure to subtract the length of the edging from the overall sleeve length before you figure your sleeve taper, so the edging can be worked without shaping.

Edging Added On

Some designers choose to add edgings to garments by picking up stitches from a selvedge, cast-on, or bind-off edge. Others like to work edgings separately and sew them in place. This is a great solution to working with different yarns and gauges. In any case, you'll need to account for the length of the edging when you determine the bodice and sleeve lengths.

If you want a ribbed edging on a bodice that's worked side to side, you'll need to pick up and knit stitches along the lower bodice edge and work the ribbing downward, as in the side-to-side version of Mary's Classic Crew (page 28). In this case, you'll want to subtract the width of the

> ### 𝒯𝒾𝓅 Sleeve Edgings
>
> Whether I knit my sleeves from the shoulders to the cuffs or from the cuffs to the shoulders, I like to add the cuff edging last. If I'm working from cuff to shoulder, I use a provisional cast-on, then pick up stitches from the provisional cast-on, work the cuffs in the opposite direction, and bind them off with an invisible bind-off. This gives me the option to lengthen or shorten my sleeve once I've assembled the sweater for a true custom fit, and I prefer the look and elasticity of an invisible bind-off edge to any type of cast-on edge at the cuff.

edging from the length of the sweater before you determine the number of stitches to cast on. To add this type of edging to a sleeve, subtract the number of inches in the edging from the overall sleeve length before you figure the sleeve taper.

To add an edging to a shaped neckline, you'll need to pick up and knit stitches around the neck opening and work the edging from the pick-up row. You can work the edging for just a few rows as in the Classic Crew, work it more rows to create a turtleneck as in Linda's One-Piece Turtleneck (page 68), or increase stitches to make a collar that folds over as in Lori's Jacob's Windows Sweater (page 68) or Sandy's Cardigan for Zylie (page 87).

You can also use edgings to add length to sweater bodies or sleeves. Simply pick up and knit stitches around the hem or sleeve and work the desired edging for the desired length. This is a nice way to extend the life of a child's sweater—make the sweater a bit wide to begin with (to allow room to grow), and add edgings to the sleeves and hem as the child gets taller.

Using a Full-Size Template

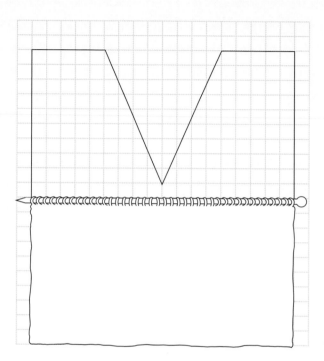

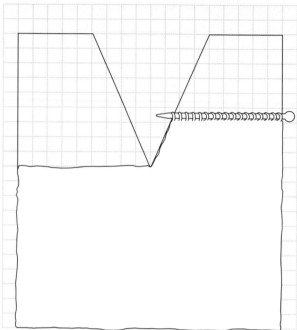

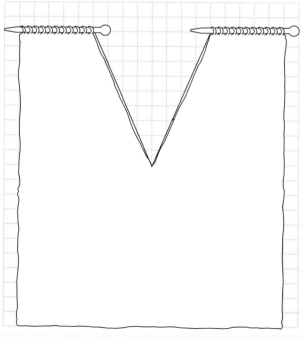

If you want to be absolutely certain to get exactly the right finished measurements, plot the sweater dimensions to scale on Pellon yardage marked with a 1" grid, (available at most fabric stores). Using the numbers in your Knitter Fitter and Sweater Map, draw the exact size and shape of your sweater pieces onto the Pellon. You can annotate the template with arrows, stitch counts, row counts, and other knitting details directly on the Pellon.

As you knit, periodically place the template on a flat surface and hold your knitting right on top of it to make sure your knitting matches your desired measurements.

When the shape of the template changes, simply work increases, decreases, cast-ons or bind-offs to make your knitting match.

Working with a template can help you expand your design skills to include sweaters worked in panels, patches, or even in free-form sections. It also can free you up from having to worry about stitch and row counts—as long as your knitted piece matches the template, you'll know that it's the right size.

Our Projects

Bouclé Boat Neck

This ultra-simple pullover illustrates how easy it is to vary the look of the Classic Crew. By choosing a handdyed bouclé yarn and knitting it at a loose gauge, I created an airy, drapey sweater that's both casual and elegant. This sweater follows the instructions for the up-and-down basic sweater, but with a boat-neck variation (that requires no neckline shaping). Textured yarns, such as this bouclé, look great knitted on larger needles, producing a fabric that is light of hand. The standard gauge for this yarn is 4 stitches per inch on size 9 (5.5 mm) needles, which would be great for a dense jacket or skirt. To get the drapey fabric I wanted in this oversized sweater, I used size 10¹/₂ (6.5 mm) needles at a gauge of just 3 stitches per inch. The resulting fabric is airy without being sheer.

Designer Notes

I handpainted four 6-ounce skeins of kid mohair bouclé from Ashland Bay in four different coordinating colorways, each successive colorway having an increasing amount of peacock blue. I balanced the "composition" by knitting large areas of different sizes in different colorways. For a painterly effect, I smoothed the transition between colorways by knitting 2 rows of each color for several inches.

Because the colorways had so many similar colors, these transitional stripes are not obvious. I used the skeins with the least amount of peacock blue at the hem and cuffs (the smallest area) and worked to the neck and shoulder line with successively bluer skeins so that most of the brilliant color frames the face.

The Fitter List for Bouclé Boat Neck

Measure your body and allow for the appropriate amount of ease (see page 14) or measure a sweater that fits the way you like and enter the numbers below. Refer to your gauge swatch for your stitch and row gauges, then translate each measurement into numbers of stitches and/or rows as you go along.

Yarn

Yarn name: **Ashland Bay Trader's Kid Mohair Bouclé**

Fiber content: **86% kid mohair, 14% nylon**

Weight classification: **Worsted (#4 Medium)**

WPI: **11**

Number of yards/pounds used: **1,290 yards; 15½ ounces**

Gauge

Stitches per inch (in stockinette stitch): **3** Rows per inch: **5½**

Needle size: **US 10½ (6.5 mm; straight)**

Details

Cast-on method: **Backward-loop**

Bind-off method: **Chain**

Selvedge treatment: **Chain stitch**

Sleeve increase/decrease method: **Paired decreases**

Seam technique: **Mattress stitch**

Notes/Variations

To minimize roll, work a row or two of single crochet (Glossary, page 134) with a size I/9 (5.5 mm) crochet hook around the hem.

Sweater Measurements

Bodice

Circumference: **54** inches

Width: **27** inches; **81** stitches

Cast-On Stitches: **81** stitches

Length With Edging: **25** inches; **138** rows

Length Without Edging: **NA**

Length of Lower Edging: **NA**

Armhole Depth: **9** inches; **50** rows

Back Neck Width Without Edging: **12** inches; **37** stitches

Back Neck Width With Edging: **NA**

Front Neck Depth Without Edging: **NA**

Front Neck Depth With Edging: **NA**

Lower Front Neck Width: **NA** inches

Begin Front Neck At: **NA**

Shoulder Width: **7½** inches; **22** stitches

Sleeves

Sleeve Length Without Edging: **14½** inches; **80** rows

Sleeve Length With Edging: **NA**

Cuff Circumference: **10½** inches; **32** stitches

Half Cuff Circumference: **5¼** inches; **16** stitches

Cuff Length: **NA**

Upper Arm Circumference: **18** inches; **54** stitches

Half Upper Arm Circumference: **9** inches; **27** stitches

Sleeve Taper Rate: **2** stitches decreased every **7** rows **11** times

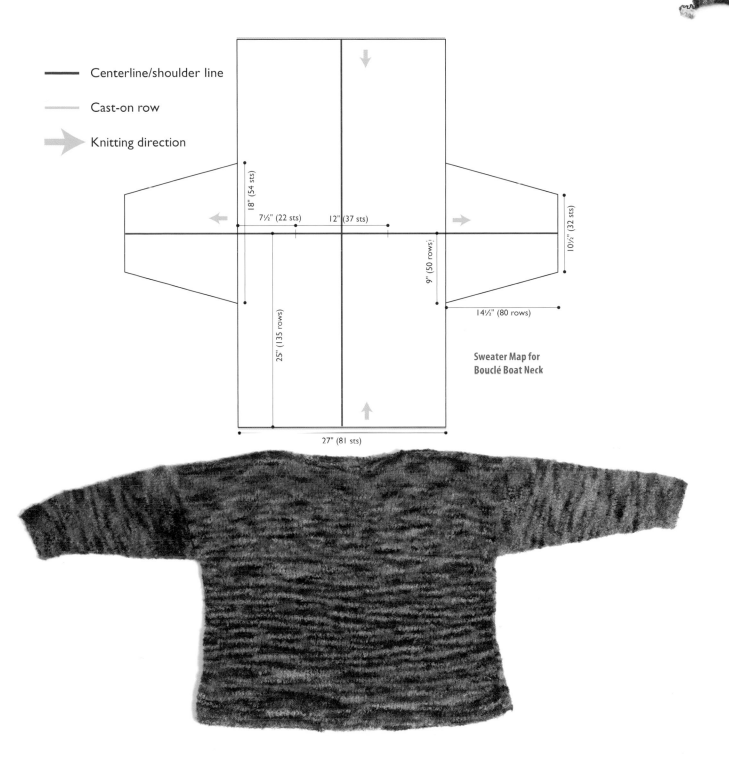

Centerline/shoulder line

Cast-on row

Knitting direction

18" (54 sts)

7½" (22 sts)

12" (37 sts)

10½" (32 sts)

9" (50 rows)

25" (135 rows)

14½" (80 rows)

Sweater Map for Bouclé Boat Neck

27" (81 sts)

1 Determine Gauge

Work as for the Up-and-Down Classic Crew (page 17).

2 Determine Bodice Circumference and Length

Work as for the Up-and-Down Classic Crew (page 17), allowing ease for an oversized fit.

3 Determine Stitch Count

Work as for the Up-and-Down Classic Crew (page 18).

4 Knit the Bodice Back

Work as for the Up-and-Down Classic Crew (page 18), using a backward-loop cast-on (Glossary, page 133) and a chain bind-off (Glossary, page 131).

5 Determine Front Neckline Width and Depth

Work as for the Up-and-Down Classic Crew (page 19), but substitute a boat-neck shaping (page 38).

6 Knit the Bodice Front

Work as for the Up-and-Down Classic Crew (page 22), using a backward-loop cast-on and a chain bind-off, and eliminating the neckline shaping to form a boat neck (page 38).

7 Determine Sleeve Dimensions

Work as for the Up-and-Down Classic Crew (page 22).

8 Determine Sleeve Taper

Work as for the Up-and-Down Classic Crew (page 24).

9 Knit the Sleeves

Work as for the Up-and-Down Classic Crew (page 26), picking up stitches around the armhole and working from shoulder to cuff, ending with a chain bind-off.

10 Join Seams

Work as for the Up-and-Down Classic Crew (page 27), using a mattress stitch.

11 Add Edgings

Eliminate this step.

12 Finishing Touches

Work as for the Up-and-Down Classic Crew (page 27).

Alina's Basketweave Coat

For this warm coat, Alina Egerman followed instructions for the basic up-and-down sweater, but lengthened the bodice, divided the front into two pieces to make a cardigan with a center overlap, shaped the armhole for a modified drop shoulder, and added a stand-up collar to the crew neckline. For a thick fabric, Alina combined a strand of her handspun with a strand of commercial yarn in a basket-weave-stitch pattern. Because of the weight of the fabric, Alina knitted the fronts and back separately, then sewed them together. To minimize bulk in the seams, she worked a mattress stitch into half of the selvedge stitches.

Designer Notes

"My project began with a silver Romney fleece carded with purple-dyed flecks of silk noil. When I finished spinning the yarn, I found that it was harsher and denser than I had originally envisioned, plus the dye in the noils bled out, blurring the contrast I loved so much. To make matters worse, I was short on yardage.

"I persevered and bought some commercial brushed mohair yarn in vibrant purple and swatched with both strands knitted together. The fabric was much more pleasant to the touch than the Romney yarn alone and much more wind- and rain-repellent than the mohair alone. Because I was knitting on larger needles now, the double-stranded yarn knitted into fewer rows per inch, requiring less handspun.

"As a spinner I am familiar with the tendency to hoard handspun yarn. But I also feel that it is important to accept and make use of what we have. The wool, the work of my hands, even my disappointment with the outcome were all spun into my yarn. By using my imagination, I was able to make something I love without letting anything go to waste."

The Fitter List for Alina's Basketweave Coat

Measure your body and allow for the appropriate amount of ease (see page 14) or measure a sweater that fits the way you like and enter the numbers below. Refer to your gauge swatch for your stitch and row gauges, then translate each measurement into numbers of stitches and/or rows as you go along.

Yarn

Yarn name: **Yarn #1: Berroco Mohair**

Fiber content: **78% mohair, 13% wool, 9% nylon**

Weight classification: **Worsted (#4 Medium)**

WPI: **12**

Number of yards/pounds used: **1,210 yards**

Yarn name: **Yarn #2: Romney Wool Handspun**

Fiber content: **80% wool, 20% silk**

Weight classification: **Sport (#2 Light)**

WPI: **14**

Number of yards/pounds used: **1,210 yards**

Gauge

Stitches per inch (in pattern stitch with both yarns held together): **4**

Rows per inch: **6**

Needle size: **U.S. size 9 (5.5 mm; straight)**

Details

Cast-on method: **Long-tail**

Bind-off method: **Chain**

Selvedge treatment: **NA (all stitches worked in pattern)**

Sleeve increase/decrease method: **Paired decreases**

Seam technique: **Modified mattress stitch**

Sweater Measurements

Bodice

Circumference: **44** inches

Width: **22** inches; **88** stitches

Length With Edging: **28** inches; **170** rows

Length Without Edging: **27** inches; **166** rows

Length of Edging: **¾** inches; **4** rows

Armhole Depth: **9** inches; **50** stitches

Back Neck Width Without Edging: **8** inches; **32** stitches

Back Neck Width With Edging: **NA**

Front Neck Depth Without Edging: **2** inches; **12** rows

Front Neck Depth With Edging: **NA**

Lower Front Neck Width: **6** inches; **24** stitches

Begin Front Neck At: **26** inches; **158** rows

Shoulder Width: **6** inches; **24** stitches

Sleeves

Sleeve Length Without Edging: **16** inches; **98** rows

Sleeve Length With Edging: **17** inches; **102** rows

Cuff Circumference: **8** inches; **32** stitches

Half Cuff Circumference: **4** inches; **16** stitches

Cuff Length: **1** inch; **4** rows

Upper Arm Circumference: **20** inches; **80** stitches

Half Upper Arm Circumference: **10** inches; **40** stitches

Sleeve Taper Rate: **1** stitch decreased each edge every **4** rows **24** times

Notes/Variations

Cardigan variation:

Bodice Front Width Including Border: 50 stitches

Center Front Overlap Width: 4 stitches

Seven 1" buttons for center front; one ⅝" button for collar. Alina worked one-stitch buttonholes on Rows 19-20, 41-42, 63-64, 85-86, 107-108, 129-130, and 151-152, centered on the 6-stitch garter stitch front edgings as follows.

Right-side row: K4, BO 1, k2.

Wrong-side row: K2, use the backward-loop method (Glossary, page 133) to increase 1 stitch, k3.

Modified Drop-Shoulder Variation (Angle Method):

Across Front Width: 20"; 80 stitches

Width of Armhole Shaping: 1"; 4 stitches

Armhole Depth after Shaping: 9"; 54 rows

Depth of Angle Shaping (angle Method): 1"; 6 rows

Overarm Sleeve Length: 18"; 108 rows

Underarm Sleeve Length: 17"; 102 rows

Sleeve Cap Length: 1"; 6 rows

Sleeve Cap Top Row Width: 18"; 72 stitches

Collar variation:

Collar picked up around neckline and worked for 4" (24 rows).

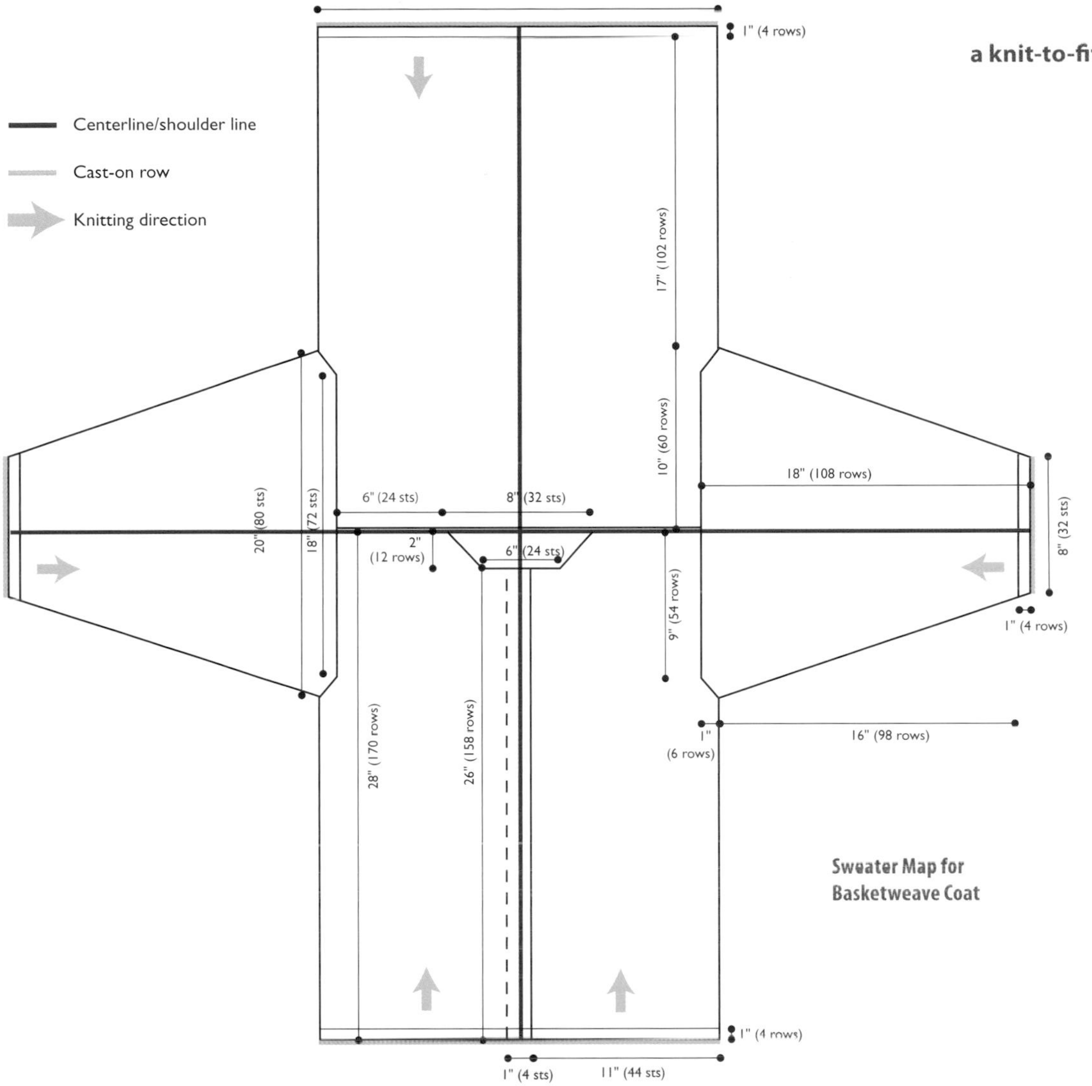

─── Centerline/shoulder line

─── Cast-on row

➜ Knitting direction

1" (4 rows)

17" (102 rows)

10" (60 rows)

18" (108 rows)

8" (32 sts)

20" (80 sts)

18" (72 sts)

6" (24 sts)

8" (32 sts)

2" (12 rows)

6" (24 sts)

9" (54 rows)

1" (4 rows)

28" (170 rows)

26" (158 rows)

1" (6 rows)

16" (98 rows)

Sweater Map for Basketweave Coat

1" (4 rows)

1" (4 sts)   11" (44 sts)

Alina combined a strand of commercial brushed mohair with her handspun yarn.

1 Determine Gauge

Work as for the Up-and-Down Classic Crew (see page 17), but determine gauge on basketweave-stitch pattern.

Basketweave Stitch (multiple of 4 stitches)

Rows 1 and 2: *K2, p2; repeat from *.
Rows 3 and 4: *P2, k2; repeat from *.
Repeat Rows 1–4 for pattern.

2 Determine Bodice Circumference and Length

Work as for the Up-and-Down Classic Crew (page 17), adding the desired length.

3 Determine Stitch Count

Work as for the Up-and-Down Classic Crew (page 18).

4 Knit the Bodice Back

Work as for the Up-and-Down Classic Crew (page 18), using a long-tail cast-on (Glossary, page 133) and beginning with 4 rows of garter stitch, then changing to basketweave-stitch pattern. Change the shoulder to a modified drop shoulder with angled shaping (page 40). Use a chain bind-off (Glossary, page 131).

Modified Drop Shoulder

Bind off 1 stitch at the base of the armhole, then decrease 1 stitch every 2 rows until all of the armhole stitches have been eliminated (leaving just the number of stitches for the desired across-front width). Work the remaining bodice straight to the shoulder line. Bind off all the stitches.

5 Determine Front Neckline Width and Depth

Work as for the Up-and-Down Classic Crew (page 19), centering the width of the front overlap (to accommodate button and buttonhole bands) along the centerline.

6 Knit the Bodice Front

Beginning with a long-tail cast-on and ending with a chain bind-off, work as a cardigan (page 37) with a 6-stitch overlap at the center front, and working buttonholes as described in the Fitter List. Work a modified drop shoulder with angled shaping to match the bodice back.

Tip **Determining Armhole Depth**

Sometimes it's easier to determine armhole depth by measuring your desired bodice length from the armhole down. Hold your arm out to the side and measure from 2" beneath the crook of your underarm to your desired hem length. Subtract that number from the total desired garment length, and the remaining number of inches is the armhole depth. Cast on the desired bodice-width stitches and knit the Bodice Back to this measurement. Measure from the top of your knitting to your shoulder line to determine your armhole depth.

Tip __Reducing Bulk in Armholes__

If you don't want the bulk of a seam under the armhole, use a stockinette selvedge on the sleeve and bodice. Work the decreases on the selvedge edges by working the first (and last) 2 stitches together. Then use a mattress stitch seam with a one-half stitch seam allowance (Glossary, page 138).

For simplicity, knit the front piece that will have the buttons first. That way you won't have to worry about buttonhole placement. When that piece is completed, use it to determine the placement of buttons and work the buttonholes on the other front piece to match (see Alina's Tip for Buttonhole Placement at right).

Work Front in Two Pieces

To make a cardigan, divide the number of stitches in the desired bodice width in half and work one half for each side of the front, working the two halves as mirror images of each other. To add bands to accommodate the buttons and buttonholes, add a few stitches to the center front of each piece. Alina wanted to work her bands in garter stitch with a 1" overlap. Because her gauge for garter stitch was tighter than her gauge for basketweave stitch, Alina worked 6 stitches to get the desired 1".

Modified Drop Shoulder

Work the modified drop shoulder to match the bodice back, remembering to work the armhole shaping on opposite sides of the two fronts so they will mirror each other.

Neckline

Work as for the Up-and-Down Classic Crew (pages 20–21), but divide the neckline chart between the two fronts. Be sure to include the stitches for the front overlap on each piece.

Indicate overlap edging on neckline graph by drawing a solid line on the half of the bodice that will fall in front (buttonhole band) and a dotted line on the half of the bodice that will fall behind (buttonband). Add the width of the plackets to the number of stitches in the bodice fronts.

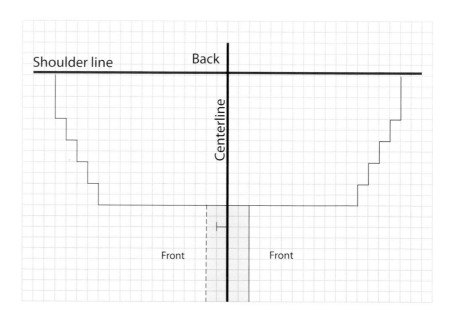

7 Determine Sleeve Dimensions

Work as for the Up-and-Down Classic Crew (page 22), but alter the shape to accommodate a modified drop shoulder with an angled notch (page 40).

8 Determine Sleeve Taper

Work as for the Up-and-Down Classic Crew (page 24), but use the underarm length (i.e., do not include the sleeve cap) for the taper calculations (see page 41).

9 Knit the Sleeves

Beginning with a long-tail cast-on and ending with a chain bind-off, work a modified drop shoulder with an angled notch (page 40). Begin with 4 rows of garter stitch, then work the basketweave-stitch pattern to the end. Work the sleeve to the desired underarm length, working the taper as you go. Shape the cap exactly as the arm hole: bind off 1 stitch, then decrease 1 stitch at each end of the needle every other row until you reach the number of stitches that corresponds to the desired width of the sleeve cap top row. Bind off all stitches on the next right-side row.

10 Join Seams

Work as for the Up-and-Down Classic Crew (page 27), using mattress stitch seams.

11 Add Edgings

Pick up and knit 1 stitch for every stitch or row around the neckline opening. Work even in basketweave stitch until the collar is the desired length. Bind off all the stitches.

12 Finishing Touches

Work as for the Up-and-Down Classic Crew (page 27). Sew buttons to left front, opposite buttonholes, saving the smaller button for the left front collar (on Alina's coat it is on Row 17, 14 stitches from the centerline). Sew a loop of yarn in the top edge of the right front collar opposite the collar button.

> ### Tip Button Placement
>
> Traditionally, buttons are sewn on the left side for women, right side for men. (I remember this by thinking of the painting of Napoleon with his right hand slipped between the buttons of his coat.) Place the buttons evenly spaced on the buttonband. Mark the placement with crossed pins. Since the buttonholes will appear between garter ridges, place the horizontal pin in the groove between the ridges and the vertical pin to mark the center of the button. Remove the buttons.
>
> To balance the button placement, decide on the exact placement for the top and bottom buttons first. Then count the rows between the pins for each button, making sure you have the same number of garter ridges between each button. If the number of rows differs between some of the buttons, begin at the top button and count down the front placket, placing the buttons at even intervals. It's better to have the bottom button a little high than the top button too low.
>
> Now place a button on the front placket again to determine the width of the buttonhole. Note that the buttonhole can stretch to nearly twice its size, so make it about a third smaller than the button. The number of stitches in this width is the number of stitches to bind off for each buttonhole.

Linda's One-Piece Turtleneck

Linda Berning modified the Up-and-Down Classic Crew by working this sweater in a single piece from the back hemline up to the shoulders and then down to the front hemline, shaping the sleeves and neckline along the way. When Linda reached the armholes of the back, she cast on her sleeve length, then shaped the sleeve taper with short-rows, working a few more stitches in each row, until she had incorporated all the stitches in the cast-on row. She then knitted straight until she reached her half-cuff circumference at the shoulder line, and reversed the process for the front. To finish, Linda picked up stitches around the neckline and worked a ribbed turtleneck. Because Linda worked the entire sweater in seed stitch, she didn't have to add a stabilizing ribbing or edging at the hem and cuffs. She chose to work a chain cast-on for the lower back edge and a chain bind-off for the lower front edge so they would have the same look and flexibility.

Designer Notes

Linda owns a knitting shop and helps customers select yarns and design sweaters on a daily basis. She asked for direction on her project to narrow her focus, so I asked her to try out a one-piece sweater.

Linda reports, "I enjoyed knitting this design because I don't like to knit sweaters in pieces. The fact that you start this sweater at the bottom, work all the way up and add in your sleeves at the same time, and work back down the other side is great! The short-rows leave a single row at the underarm seam . . . so easy to sew up. And it's reversible! One piece! This is definitely my style of sweater."

Linda chose to knit this sweater with Manos del Uruguay yarn because it looks so much like handspun (and she carries a lot of it in her shop). She choose seed stitch because it looks good, needs no edging, and helps hide some of those thin spots in unevenly spun yarn.

The Fitter List for Linda's One-Piece Turtleneck

Measure your body and allow for the appropriate amount of ease (see page 14) or measure a sweater that fits the way you like and enter the numbers below. Refer to your gauge swatch for your stitch and row gauges, then translate each measurement into numbers of stitches and/or rows as you go along.

Yarn

Yarn name: __Manos del Uruguay Wool__

Fiber content: __100% wool__

Weight classification: __Worsted (#4 Medium)__

WPI: __11__

Number of yards/pounds used: __1,125 yards__

Gauge

Stitches per inch (in seed stitch): __4__ Rows per inch: __7__

Needle size: __US size 9 (5.5 mm; 16" and 36" or longer circular)__

Hook size: __H/8 (4.75 mm)__

Details

Cast-on method: __Chain__

Bind-off method: __Chain__

Selvedge treatment: __None__

Sleeve increase/decrease method: __Short rows__

Seam technique: __Mattress stitch for side seam; fishbone stitch for underarm seam__

> *Tip* __Matching Cast-ons and Bind-offs__
> Whenever I knit something side to side, I like to pair methods of casting on and binding off (see Glossary, pages 131–134) that look and feel the same. Scarves and shrugs look best when the cast-on edge matches the bind-off edge. On sweaters knitted side to side, these edges meet at the side seams, and if the cast-on matches the bind-off, the seams will be smooth and uniform.

Sweater Measurements

Bodice

Circumference: __44__ inches

Width: __22__ inches; __88__ stitches

Cast-On Stitches: __88__ stitches

Length With Edging: __21__ inches; __148__ rows

Length Without Edging: __NA__

Length of Lower Edging: __NA__

Armhole Depth: __10__ inches; __70__ rows

Back Neck Width Without Edging: __7__ inches; __28__ stitches

Back Neck Width With Edging: __NA__

Front Neck Depth Without Edging: __2³/₄__ inches; __19__ rows

Front Neck Depth With Edging: __NA__

Lower Front Neck Width: __4¹/₂__ inches; __18__ stitches

Begin Front Neck At: __18¹/₄__ inches; __128__ rows

Shoulder Width: __7¹/₂__ inches; __30__ stitches

Sleeves

Sleeve Length Without Edging: __NA__

Sleeve Length With Edging: __18__ inches; __72__ stitches

Cuff Circumference: __7¹/₂__ inches; __52__ rows

Half Cuff Circumference: __3³/₄__ inches; __26__ rows

Cuff Length: __NA__

Upper Arm Circumference: __20__ inches; __140__ rows

Half Upper Arm Circumference: __10__ inches; __70__ rows

Sleeve Taper Rate: __Add/subtract 3 stitches every 2 rows 22 times__

Notes/Variations

Turtleneck length: 2¹/₂"; 18 rounds

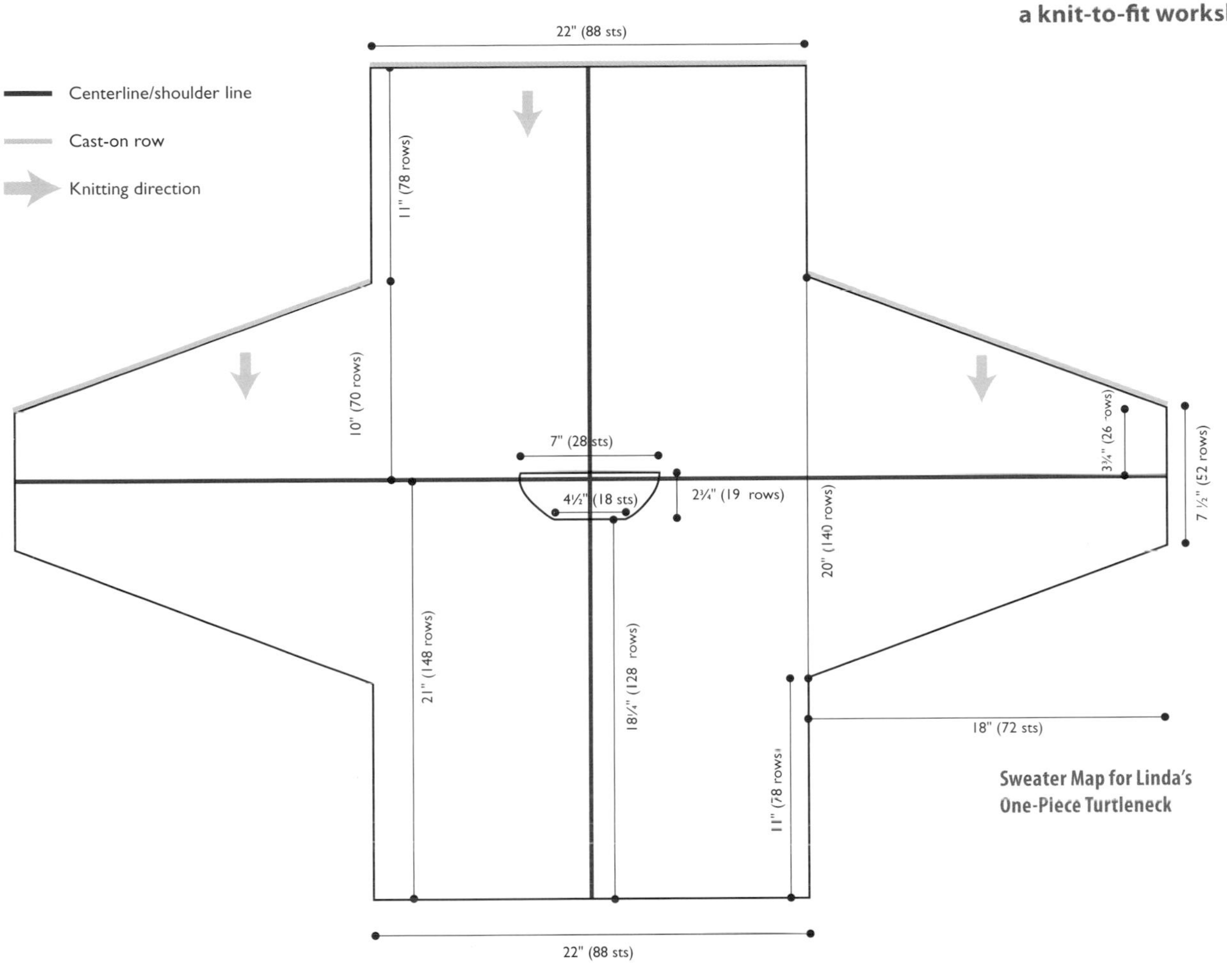

Centerline/shoulder line

Cast-on row

Knitting direction

22" (88 sts)

11" (78 rows)

10" (70 rows)

7" (28 sts)

4½" (18 sts)

2¾" (19 rows)

3¼" (26 rows)

7½" (52 rows)

20" (140 rows)

21" (148 rows)

18¼" (128 rows)

11" (78 rows)

18" (72 sts)

**Sweater Map for Linda's
One-Piece Turtleneck**

22" (88 sts)

1 Determine Gauge

Work as for the Up-and-Down Classic Crew (page 17), but use a seed-stitch pattern.

Seed Stitch

Row 1: *K1, p1; rep from *, end k1 if there is an odd number of stitches.
Row 2: Knit the purls and purl the knits.
Repeat Row 2 for pattern.

2 Determine Bodice Circumference and Length

Work as for the Up-and-Down Classic Crew (page 17).

3 Determine Stitch Count

Work as for the Up-and-Down Classic Crew (page 18).

4 Knit the Bodice Back

Beginning with a chain cast-on (Glossary, page 133) and ending with a chain bind-off (Glossary, page 131), work as for the Up-and-Down Classic Crew (page 18), but

> ### Tip Measuring Pieces with Live Stitches
>
> If you work this sweater on straight needles, you'll have a hard time using your fabric piece for measuring purposes without removing the stitches from the needles. Of course, you'd put your fabric on waste yarn, but that means you'd have to put it back on the needles later.
>
> Instead, find a circular needle whose cable is longer than your row of live stitches—the needle size should be the same or smaller than the one you're working with. Transfer these stitches to the circular needle (or two shorter circular needles, putting half of the stitches on one and half on the other). Secure a rubber band around each pointed end of the needle to prevent the stitches from slipping off.
>
> When you're through using the fabric for measuring purposes, just knit your next row right off the circular needle and you're back in business.

substitute seed-stitch pattern and work only to base of armhole. Go to Step 7 to determine the sleeve dimensions and Step 8 to determine the sleeve taper. Work the back half of the sleeves as a continuation of the bodice back as described in Step 9 until the back measures the desired length to the shoulder line.

5 Determine Front Neckline Width and Depth

Work as for the Up-and-Down Classic Crew (page 19).

6 Knit the Bodice Front

Work from top down on live stitches from the bodice back, beginning at the shoulder line and working downward to the front hemline, working from the neckline chart from the top down, reversing the sleeve shaping along the way, and ending with a chain bind-off.

Shape Neckline

When you've completed the bodice back, determine placement of the neck opening by marking the center back. Use a removable marker or piece of waste yarn to mark the center stitch (if you have an odd number of stitches) or space between 2 stitches (if you have an even number of stitches) on your needles. Place additional markers each side of this center marker to denote the desired number of stitches in the back neck width without edging, centered on the center marker. (You may want to use different colored markers here to distinguish them from the markers between the bodice and sleeve stitches.) On the next row, bind off the stitches between the neckline markers (removing the markers when you come to them). Turn the neckline chart upside down so you can follow it as you work the neck downward from the shoulder. Following

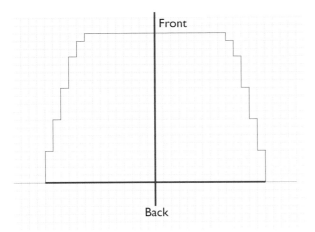

Front

Back

Linda's neckline opening is knitted from the shoulder line down. Bind off the neckline width at the shoulder line, then work the two sides separately: Knit straight for 4 rows, work a single increase at the neck edge, [work straight for 3 rows, increase at neck edge on next row] 3 times, work 1 row, increase at neck edge on next row—5 increases total in 19 rows. Cast on stitches for the front neck width to join the two sides.

the chart in its upside-down orientation, shape each side of the neck separately, and rejoin the two sides by using the backward-loop method (Glossary, page 133) to cast on the appropriate number of stitches at the lower front neck. Continue to front hemline, working the front half of the sleeves as described in Step 9, then proceed to Step 10.

7 Determine Sleeve Dimensions

Work as for the Up-and-Down Classic Crew (page 22).

8 Determine Sleeve Taper

Mark the sleeve dimensions on the partially knitted bodice back as for the Up-and-Down Classic Crew (page 24), but orient the sleeve so that rows of knitting are parallel to the length of the sleeve. The number of stitches along line AB will be the number of stitches to cast on for the sleeve. The number of rows in line AC will be the number of rows in the armhole (and the half upper arm circumfer-

ence). The number of rows in line BD will be the number of rows in the half cuff circumference.

Plot the sleeve on graph paper and draw the taper line as for the Up-and-Down Classic Crew (page 27), but instead of marking dots at every point where the taper crosses a horizontal line of the graph paper, mark dots where the taper line crosses every second horizontal row (because the short-row sleeve shaping will be worked on alternate rows). Linda's taper rate is 3 stitches every 2 rows.

9 Knit the Sleeves
Back Half of Sleeves

Beginning with a right-side row, place a marker before the first stitch of the bodice back, then use the chain method to cast on the appropriate number of stitches for the total sleeve length. With the right side of the work still facing, knit these new stitches, then work across all the back stitches. Place another marker after the last stitch of the bodice back, then working on the wrong side, use the chain method to cast on the same number of sleeve stitches as before. You will now have all of the stitches for the bodice back and both sleeves on the same needle (this is why you need a long circular needle).

To work a 3-stitch taper in short-rows, work 3 more

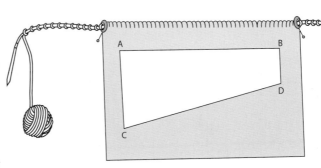

A   B

C   D

Determine sleeve measurements on the partially knitted bodice back.

of the stitches every 2 rows (i.e., work the first 3 sleeve sts on the first pair of rows, then work the first 6 sleeve stitches on the next pair of rows, then work the first 9 sleeve stitches on the next pair, and so on). To maintain a smooth transition between the 3-stitch groups, you'll work a short-row "wrap and turn" (Glossary, page 140) on the last stitch of each group by working to the last stitch of the group, bringing the yarn to the front, slipping the last stitch, returning the yarn to the back, and turning the work. When you come to the wrapped stitch on a following row, lift the wrap onto the right needle and work it together with the wrapped stitch.

Here's how it works for Linda's sweater: Work in seed stitch across the newly cast-on stitches of the second sleeve to the marker, work in established pattern to the next marker, work 2 stitches of the first sleeve, wrap the 3rd stitch, and turn the work. Work in pattern to the second marker, work 2 stitches of the second sleeve, wrap the next stitch, and turn the work.

Continue in this manner, working 2 sts past the wrapped stitch, wrap the 3rd stitch, and turn the work, until 6 stitches remain at the end of each sleeve. Work even in pattern across all stitches until you reach the shoulder line of the bodice and the Half Cuff Circumference at the ends of the sleeves. Mark the first stitch of the row to denote the shoulder line.

Front Half of Sleeves

After finishing the neckline shaping, work straight until you've worked 2 rows less than the desired number of rows in the cuff circumference (so that the short-row taper will end with 2 full-length rows). There should be the same number of straight rows worked before and after the shoulder marker.

Begin working short-rows again to taper the front half of each sleeve. Knit across the first row to the last 7 stitches, wrap the next stitch, then turn the work (6 stitches remain unworked at the cuff edge). Knit to the last 7 stitches of the next row, wrap the next stitch, and turn. On subsequent rows, work to 3 stitches before the wrapped stitch of the previous row, wrap the next stitch, then turn the work. Continue in this fashion until all of the sleeve stitches remain unworked. On the last rows, you'll wrap the stitch next to the markers between the sleeve and bodice. Work in pattern across all stitches for 2 rows. Bind off all the sleeve stitches at the beginning of the next row, then work across the bodice stitches and remaining sleeve stitches. On the next row, use the chain method to bind off the remaining sleeve stitches—just the stitches for the front bodice will remain.

10 Join Seams

Work as for the Up-and-Down Classic Crew (page 27), using a mattress stitch for garter selvedge (Glossary, page 138) to join the seed stitches along the side seams and a fishbone stitch (Glossary, page 136) to join the sleeve seams.

11 Add Edgings

Using a short (16") circular needle or set of double-pointed needles, pick up and knit stitches around the neck opening at a rate of 1 stitch per stitch/row, adjusting the number of stitches if necessary to have a multiple of 4 stitches. Work in knit 2, purl 2 ribbing in rounds until the turtleneck is the desired length.

12 Finishing Touches

Work as for the Up-and-Down Classic Crew (page 27).

Knitting a Sweater in One Piece (up and down)

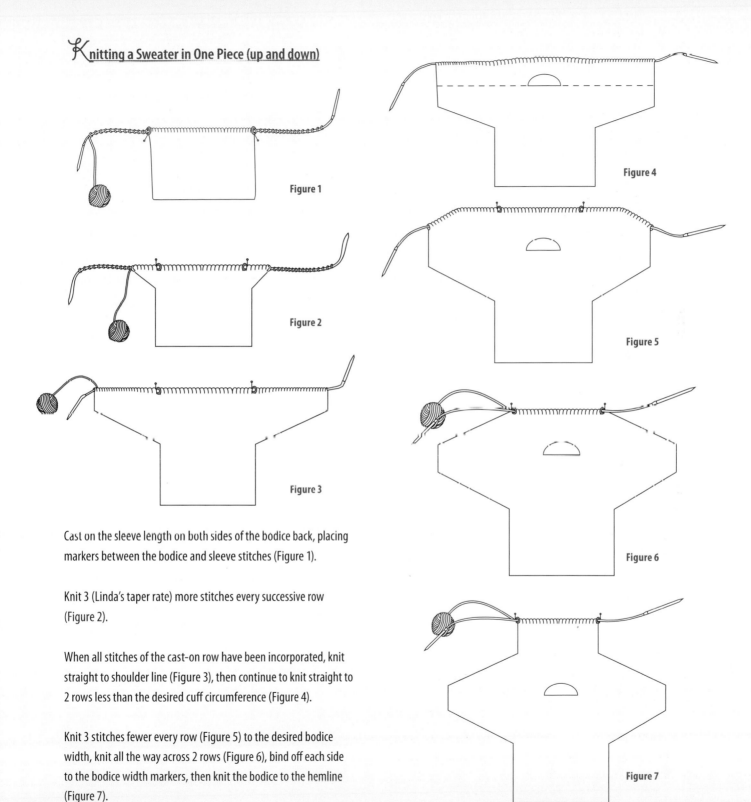

Figure 1

Figure 2

Figure 3

Figure 4

Figure 5

Figure 6

Figure 7

Cast on the sleeve length on both sides of the bodice back, placing markers between the bodice and sleeve stitches (Figure 1).

Knit 3 (Linda's taper rate) more stitches every successive row (Figure 2).

When all stitches of the cast-on row have been incorporated, knit straight to shoulder line (Figure 3), then continue to knit straight to 2 rows less than the desired cuff circumference (Figure 4).

Knit 3 stitches fewer every row (Figure 5) to the desired bodice width, knit all the way across 2 rows (Figure 6), bind off each side to the bodice width markers, then knit the bodice to the hemline (Figure 7).

Lori's Jacob's Windows Sweater

Lori Lawson designed this cardigan for her coastal Southern California climate. Following the lines of the Up-and-Down Classic Crew, she divided the front bodice in half to make a cardigan. To keep the sweater from being too warm, she designed the front without an overlap and the sleeves three-quarter length. The shoulders are shaped at a natural angle and the neckline is carved a little wider and deeper than a crewneck and is finished off with a foldover collar. Lori simplified the bodice by knitting it in one piece up to the armholes, eliminating the need for side seams. She knitted the deep sleeves in the round, alternating bands (and colors) of stockinette stitch, garter stitch, and seed stitch.

Designer Notes

"Jacob's Windows was my maiden voyage into designing as well as knitting with my own handspun and handdyed yarn. In previous years I knitted many sweaters with commercial yarns and patterns, but when I learned to spin I found a new passion.

"At our local zoo on shearing day, the shearer saw me spinning and gave me some of the newly shorn hoggit fleece of a Jacob lamb. I was so excited; I washed, carded, and spun it within days. Lacking enough to knit a whole sweater, I searched my stash of handdyed handspun Columbia I had been hoarding for who knows what, and the idea of using the Jacob's yarn as a backdrop for windows of colored yarns was born.

"I really didn't plan this sweater out as carefully as it sounds. I had a picture in my mind and just started knitting. When I ran out of Jacob's yarn partway into the sleeve, I abandoned my plan to extend the windows into the sleeve. When I ran out of the colors I used in the body of the sweater, I handpainted a roving in some of the same colors I'd used to dye those yarns.

"I purposefully did not overlap the front bodice but made loop buttonholes that would cross over to the buttons. I knitted three-quarter sleeves because I am always pushing up my sleeves anyway. These sleeves sit right where I would have pushed them up."

$\mathcal{T}$he Fitter List for Lori's Jacob's Windows Sweater

Measure your body and allow for the appropriate amount of ease (see page 14) or measure a sweater that fits the way you like and enter the numbers below. Refer to your gauge swatch for your stitch and row gauges, then translate each measurement into numbers of stitches and/or rows as you go along.

Yarn

Yarn name: __Lori's handspun two-ply and singles__

Fiber content: __Columbia and Jacob wools__

Weight classification: __Worsted (#4 Medium)__

WPI: __11__

Number of yards/pounds used: __630 yards of gray heather; 150 yards of variegated (100 yards each of 4 contrasting colors); 80 yards of white__

Gauge

__Bodice:__ Stitches per inch (in charted pattern): __4.75__ Rows per inch: __5.7__

__Sleeve:__ Stitches per inch (in stockinette stitch and garter stitch): __4.76__

Rows per inch (averaged between stocinette stitch and garter stitch): __7.69__

Needle size: __US size 8 (5.5 mm; 36" or longer circular)__

Details

Cast-on method: __Long-tail__

Bind-off method: __Chain__

Selvedge treatment: __Stockinette stitch__

Sleeve increase/decrease method: __Paired decreases__

Seam technique: __NA (stitches picked up, not seamed)__

Notes/Variations

Work fronts and back as a single piece: To avoid side seams, cast for the full bodice circumference and work the fronts and back in a single piece to the armhole. At the armhole, divide the fronts and back and work each separately to the shoulders.

Cardigan variation: Five ³/₄" buttons; single crochet loops sewn to left front for buttonholes
Bodice Front Width (One Half Bodice) Without Edging: 10¹/₂"; 50 stitches
Center Front Overlap Width: 0"
Center Front Borders: 1"; 10 rows garter stitch (worked sideways)
Shaped Shoulders: Begin Shoulder Shaping At: 118 rows (including border). Work shaping in three groups: 10 stitches, 10 stitches, 9 stitches
Collar variation: Collar picked up around neckline at a rate of 5 stitches for every 4 stitches/rows and worked in garter stitch for 2" (18 rows). Collar edged with picot crochet.

Sweater Measurements

Bodice

Circumference: __45__ inches; __205__ stitches (without front edgings)

Width: __22__ inches; __105__ stitches

Cast-On Stitches: __205__ stitches

Length With Edging: __21__ inches; __124__ rows

Length Without Edging: __NA__

Length of Lower Edging: __1__ inches; __10__ rows

Armhole Depth: __10¹/₂__ inches; __60__ rows

Back Neck Width Without Edging: __10__ inches; __47__ stitches

Back Neck Width With Edging: __NA__

Front Neck Depth Without Edging: __4__ inches; __24__ rows
  (includes 5 rows of shoulder shaping)

Front Neck Depth With Edging: __NA__

Lower Front Neck Width: __4__ inches (includes edging)

Begin Front Neck At: __17__ inches; __102__ rows (includes edging)

Shoulder Width: __6__ inches; __29__ stitches

Sleeves

Sleeve Length Without Edging: __13__ inches; __100__ rows

Sleeve Length With Edging: __14__ inches; __110__ rows

Cuff Circumference: __9__ inches; __44__ stitches

Half Cuff Circumference: __4¹/₂__ inches; __22__ rows

Cuff Length: __1__ inches; __10__ rows

Upper Arm Circumference: __21__ inches; __100__ stitches

Half Upper Arm Circumference: __10¹/₂__ inches; __50__ stitches

Sleeve Taper Rate: __2 stitches decreased alternating every 3 rows, then every 4 rows 28 times (i.e., *work a pair of decreases on the 3rd row, work the next pair of decreases on the 4th row after that; repeat from * until 28 sets of decrease rows are completed)__

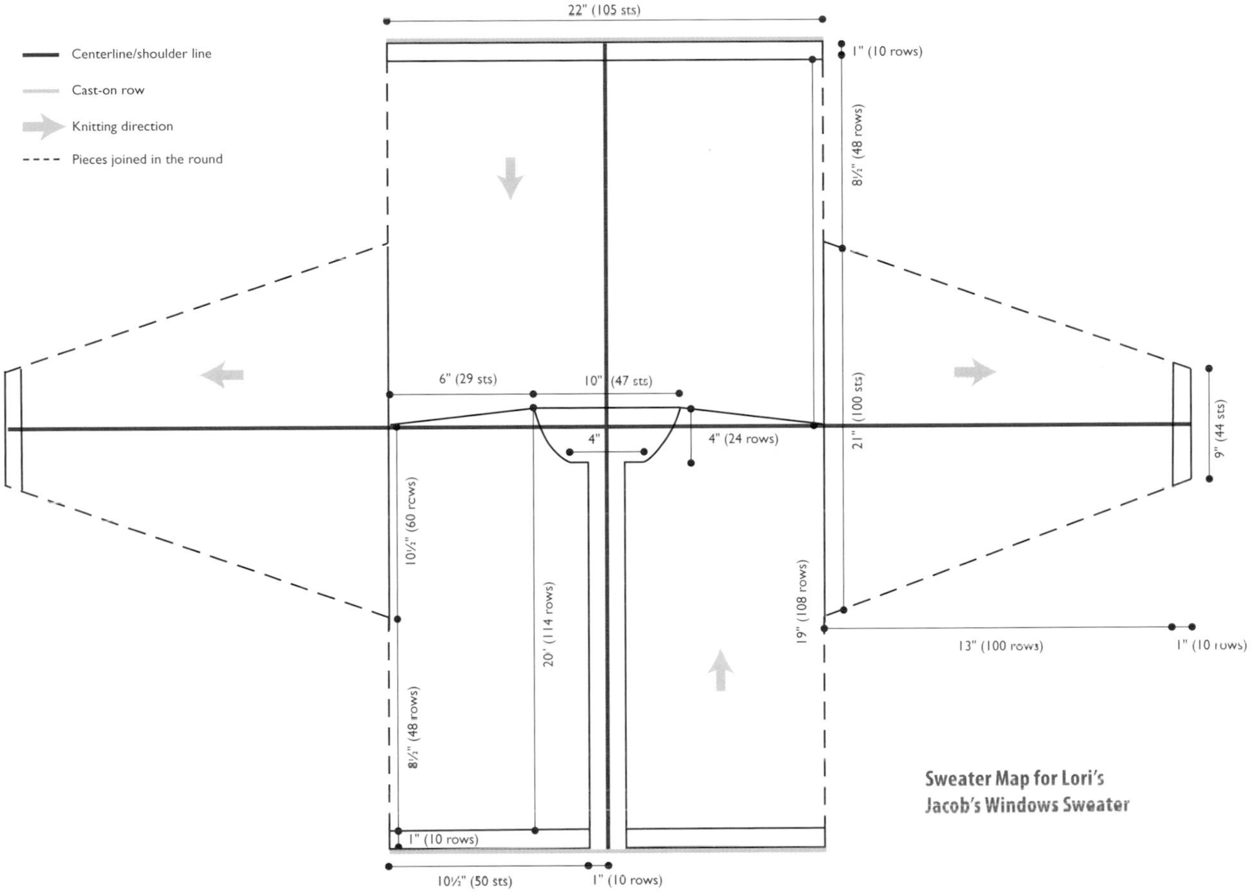

Centerline/shoulder line

Cast-on row

Knitting direction

Pieces joined in the round

22" (105 sts)

1" (10 rows)

8½" (48 rows)

6" (29 sts)

10" (47 sts)

4"

4" (24 rows)

21" (100 sts)

9" (44 sts)

10½" (60 rows)

20" (114 rows)

19" (108 rows)

13" (100 rows)

1" (10 rows)

8½" (48 rows)

1" (10 rows)

10½" (50 sts)

1" (10 rows)

**Sweater Map for Lori's
Jacob's Windows Sweater**

Windows

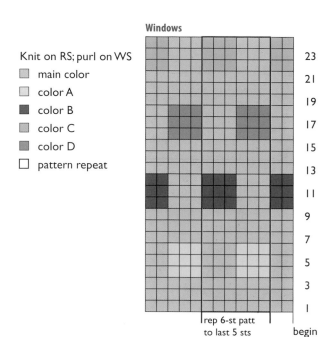

Knit on RS; purl on WS

- ▨ main color
- ▢ color A
- ■ color B
- ▨ color C
- ▨ color D
- ☐ pattern repeat

23
21
19
17
15
13
11
9
7
5
3
1

rep 6-st patt
to last 5 sts   begin

1 Determine Gauge

Work as for the Up-and-Down Classic Crew (page 17), but determine gauge for bodice according to Windows chart at left. Determine gauge for sleeves in seed stitch.

2 Determine Bodice Circumference and Length

Work as for the Up-and-Down Classic Crew (page 17).

3 Determine Stitch Count

Work as for the Up-and-Down Classic Crew (page 18), but include both fronts and back in a single piece with the cardigan opening along the center front. Lori subtracted 2″ from her desired bodice circumference (to allow for center front edging she planned to knit later from side to side) to get the number of stitches to cast on for both fronts and back. She rounded this to an odd number so she could center a 3-stitch square at the center back and end the left front with a half repeat to mirror the right front.

4 Knit the Bodice Back and Bodice Fronts

Work the bodice back and two fronts in a single piece to the armholes, then split the pieces and work the back and fronts separately to the shoulders.

Knit the Lower Back and Fronts

Using the long-tail method (Glossary, page 133) cast on stitches for the entire bodice circumference. Work as for the Up-and-Down Classic Crew (page 18) to the armholes, beginning with 1″ of garter stitch edging in white, then changing to the Windows chart with heathered gray for the background color and varying contrast colors as specified on the chart. Center the charted pattern as described at left.

Tip **Centering the Pattern on the Sweater**

The Windows chart (above) that Lori used for this sweater repeats over 6 stitches. In order to center her design over the center back, Lori needed to add 3 stitches to the end of the pattern (making the repeat a multiple of 6 stitches plus 3). The pattern repeats over 24 rows, alternating 3 rows of main color followed by 3 rows of window pattern worked in one of four contrasting colors against the main color. Lori changed the contrasting color for each window band, working the four colors in the same order to the shoulders. She worked the shoulder shaping in the main color to avoid working partial blocks of color.

To center the pattern on her sweater, Lori subtracted 3 from her total number of stitches (this is the 3-stitch square she used to center the pattern on the Bodice Back), then she divided the remaining stitches by 6 (the number of stitches in each pattern repeat). Lori had 4 stitches left over, so these became 2-stitch partial squares at the beginning and the end of each pattern row (i.e. the center front edges). The first row of pattern was worked as follows: K2 with main color, *k3 with appropriate contrasting color, k3 with main color; repeat from * to last 5 stitches, k3 with appropriate contrasting color, k2 with main color.

Divide for Armholes

Lay the knitting on a flat surface and fold the fronts on top of the back along the side "seams" so that the front selvedges are 2" apart (to compensate for the center front edging to be added later). The front and back will split at the folds—count the stitches for each front (Lori had 50 stitches—she wanted her front to be slightly larger than the back so that the front wouldn't have a tendency to gap) and the stitches for the back (Lori had 105 stitches) to make sure the folds are centered at the sides. The center back square should be at the exact center of the bodice. Place the stitches for each front on a holder to work separately later.

Knit the Upper Back

Working the back stitches only, continue to the desired bodice length to shoulders.

Shape Shoulders

Determine the number of stitches that correspond to the desired back neck width. Use markers to mark these stitches centered on the bodice back. The stitches outside these markers are the shoulder stitches. To shape the shoulders, use the chain method (Glossary, page 131) to bind off the shoulder stitches in three steps, beginning at the armhole edge (to minimize the stair-step effect,

see the tip in the Glossary, page 132). Lori had 29 stitches for each shoulder, so she bound of 10 stitches in the first two groups, then she bound off the remaining 9 stitches. Here's how it worked for each shoulder:

Row 1: (begins at armhole edge) Bind off 10 stitches, work to end—19 stitches remain.

Row 2: Work even.

Row 3: Bind off 10 stitches, work to end—9 stitches remain.

Row 4: Work even.

Row 5: Bind off remaining 9 stitches.

Determine Front Neckline Width and Depth

Work as for the Up-and-Down Classic Crew (page 19), but instead of drawing a straight line for the shoulder line, include the 5 rows of shoulder shaping as described above.

Knit the Upper Fronts

Working the bodice front in two pieces as established, continue in pattern to the base of the neckline. Shape the neckline and shoulders following your neckline graph.

Neckline

Work as for the Up-and-Down Classic Crew (page 19), but work each front separately.

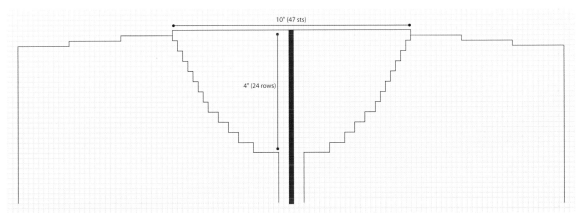

10" (47 sts)

4" (24 rows)

Neckline Chart for Lori's Jacob's Window

Shaped Shoulders

Shape the shoulders as for the Bodice Back.

7 Determine Sleeve Dimensions

Work as for the Up-and-Down Classic Crew (page 22), measuring for three-quarter-length sleeves.

8 Determine Sleeve Taper

Work as for the Up-and-Down Classic Crew (page 24).

9 Knit the Sleeves

First, join the shoulder seams with a mattress stitch for bind-off edges (Glossary, page 138). Work the sleeves as for the Up-and-Down Classic Crew (page 26), picking up and knitting stitches around the bodice and working downward to the cuff, according to the taper rate. Lori knitted the sleeves in the round (page 43), alternating 1" bands of stockinette stitch and garter stitch, and changed colors with each band, for a total of 8 bands. Then she worked seed stitch in her variegated handspun singles to her desired sleeve length without edging. Along the way, she paired her decreases on each side of a marker at the underarm seam according to her taper rate, and ended with a chain bind-off. Combining different stitch patterns in the sleeves worked for Lori because the stitch gauge was similar for all stitches. However, the row gauge did vary with stitch pattern, so she needed to rely on actual length measurements rather than numbers of rows to make her sleeves the desired length.

10 Join Seams

Because Lori knitted the fronts and back in one piece and picked up the sleeves from the armholes and worked them in the round to the cuffs, there were no seams to sew.

11 Add Edgings
Front Bands

With white, pick up and knit stitches along each front selvedge edge. To determine the number of stitches to pick up along the fronts, Lori measured the length of her center front edges (17"), then counted the number of stitches in that length along the garter stitch edging she'd already knitted along the hemline. Pick up this number of stitches evenly spaced along the length of the center front and work the edging sideways in garter stitch for 1". Bind off all the stitches.

Collar

Pick up and knit stitches around the neckline opening. To make the collar wider then the neckline opening so that the collar would fold over and lie flat, Lori picked up an extra stitch every 4 stitches around the opening. To make the collar curve even more, after she had knitted 6 rows, Lori use the lifted method (Glossary, page 135) to increase 1 stitch at each shoulder line every other row until she reached her desired collar length.

Lori finished the collar with a decorative crochet edging in a contrasting color at a repeat of 4 stitches plus 1 as follows (Glossary, page 134): Single crochet into first stitch of bind-off row, *chain 5, single crochet into 4th bind-off stitch; repeat from * to last 4 stitches, chain 5, single crochet into last bind-off stitch.

12 Finishing Touches

Work as for the Up-and-Down Classic Crew (page 27). Sew buttons to left front; sew single crochet button loops to right front.

Rectangle Vest

This simple side-to-side vest is a cardigan variation of a modified drop shoulder sweater with a boat neck and no sleeves. The fronts fold down at the neck, giving a V shape to the neckline. Instead of knitting the entire back from side seam to side seam as in the Side-to-Side Classic Crew, I knitted the back in two halves, beginning with a provisional cast-on along the centerline. Each front is worked from the center, beginning with the overlapping seed stitch edgings, outward to the side seams. This way, the bind-off edges for the fronts and back are all aligned at the sides so they will behave similarly in the seams. For simplicity, the edgings are knitted as part of the front and back fabric. The fronts close with a single button at the top of the overlapping seed stitch bands.

Designer Notes

Originally inspired by the armhole shaping of Mary Kaiser's Daisy Stitch Vest (page 127), I designed this vest for the beginning knitter. It is just rectangles without any shaping. At the time, I had no idea how valuable this pattern would become. I've used it as a template for vests and jackets ever since (for example, the Autumn Vest on page 126). Now I don't even have to think if I'm knitting with a worsted weight yarn…I just cast on 95 stitches and start knitting, and I know it's going to work out.

I find that when I cast on at the center back and work in both directions, I can knit to fit much more easily than when I cast on at the side seam. Working from the center out lets me shape my armholes after I have knitted most of the body, so I can rip them out easily if they aren't right.

I chose La Lana Wool Streakers because it has been a favorite of mine for years. I began my designing career with La Lana's Forever Random Blends and any of them would look amazing in this vest.

$\mathcal{T}$he Fitter List for Rectangle Vest

Measure your body and allow for the appropriate amount of ease (see page 14) or measure a sweater that fits the way you like and enter the numbers below. Refer to your gauge swatch for your stitch and row gauges, then translate each measurement into numbers of stitches and/or rows as you go along. Note that the direction you knit the sweater pieces (up and down or side to side) will determine whether you follow the stitch or row numbers (you only need to fill in the appropriate blank).

Yarn

Yarn name: __La Lana Wools Streakers (200 yards/skein): Silverstreak, 4 skeins__

Fiber content: __100% wool__

Weight classification: __Worsted (#4 Medium)__

WPI: __11__

Number of yards/pounds used: __800__

Gauge

Stitches per inch (in stockinette stitch): __4.33__ Rows per inch: __6.5__

Stitches per inch (in seed stitch and garter stitch): __4.25__

Rows per inch: __7.5__

Needle size: __US size 9 (5.5 mm; straight)__

Details

Cast-on method: __Provisional for bodice back; long-tail for bodice fronts__

Bind-off method: __Chain__

Selvedge treatment: __Garter stitch for lower border; chain stitch for shoulder edge__

Sleeve increase/decrease method: __NA__

Seam technique: __Mattress stitch for shoulder seams; crochet chain stitch for side seams__

Sweater Measurements

Bodice

Circumference: __39__ inches

Width (excluding overlaps): __19½__ inches; __116__ rows

Cast-On Stitches (including selvedge stitches): __95__ stitches

Length With Edging: __22__ inches; __95__ stitches

Length Without Edging: __NA__

Length of Lower Edging: __1¼__ inches; __5__ stitches

Armhole Depth: __10__ inches; __42__ stitches

Back Neck Width Without Edging: __8__ inches; __48__ rows

Back Neck Width With Edging: __NA__

Front Neck Depth Without Edging: __9__ inches; __38__ stitches

Front Neck Depth With Edging: __NA__

Lower Front Neck Width: __0__ inches

Shoulder Width: __3½__ inches; __21__ rows

Sleeves

No sleeves.

Notes/Variations

Cardigan Variation: Width of Front Overlap: 1³/₄"; 12 rows. Length of Front Overlap: 13"; 56 stitches. Width of Center Front Garter Stitch Border: 8 rows.

Modified Drop Shoulder: Across Front (or Back), between armholes: 15"; 90 rows. Width of Armhole Shaping: 14 rows. Back Width from Centerline to Shoulder: 45 rows.

Slit Along Side Seam: Length of Side Seam Slit: 3"; 13 stitches.

Boat Neck: Half Back Neck Width Without Edging: 4"; 24 rows

$\mathcal{T}ip$ **Vest Map:**
Indicate seed- and garter-stitch patterns on your sweater map by shading the appropriate areas with separate colors that represent individual stitch patterns.

Centerline/shoulder line

Cast-on row

Knitting Direction

Garter stitch

Seed stitch

Sweater Map for Rectangle Vest

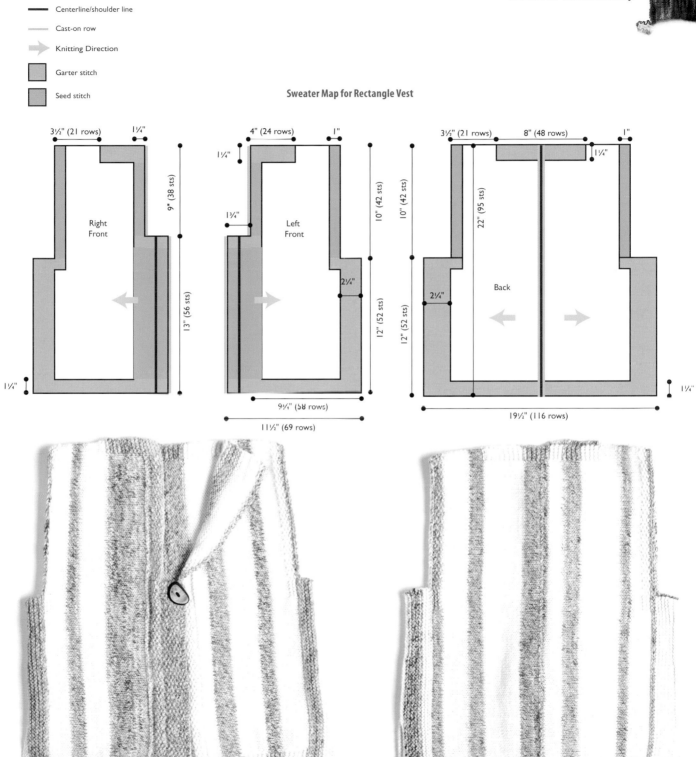

Right Front

3½" (21 rows) 1¼"

9" (38 sts)

13" (56 sts)

1¼"

Left Front

4" (24 rows) 1"

1¼"

10" (42 sts)

1¾"

2¼"

12" (52 sts)

9¼" (58 rows)

11½" (69 rows)

Back

3½" (21 rows) 8" (48 rows) 1"

1¼"

22" (95 sts)

10" (42 sts)

2¼"

12" (52 sts)

1¼"

19½" (116 rows)

1 Determine Gauge

Work as for the Up-and-Down Classic Crew (page 17).

2 Determine Bodice Circumference and Length

Work as for the Up-and-Down Classic Crew (page 17).

3 Determine Stitch Count

Work as for the Side-to-Side Classic Crew (page 18).

4 Knit the Bodice Back

Use a provisional cast-on (Glossary, page 134) at the center back and work each half to the side seams, adjusting for a boat neck (page 38) and modified drop-shoulder shaping (page 40), and working the edgings along with the bodice (page 44).

Determine Number of Stitches for Edgings

Determine the number of cast-on stitches that will be worked in the edging pattern. For this vest, I wanted about 1¹/₄" in garter stitch for noncurling edges at the hemline and neckline. At my gauge, this translated to 5 stitches. As I knitted the first row, I placed markers 5 stitches in from each edge to remind me to work those stitches in garter stitch. I worked garter stitch at the shoulder-line edging for one-half of the neckline opening, then discontinued the garter stitch at the shoulder line but continued it at the hemline all the way to the underarm panels.

Determine Width of Boat Neck

Stand in front of a mirror and use a ruler to measure the desired horizontal width of your neck opening, keeping in mind that the neckline of the bodice fronts will fold back at this width. I chose an 8" width, which corresponded to where the curve of my neck met my shoulders. Because the back is worked in two pieces from the centerline, work to one-half this width, or 4". Discontinue working the 5 edging stitches at the neck edge and work these stitches in stockinette stitch until the piece measures 1" less than half of the across-front measurements (to account for modified drop shoulder shaping, page 40).

Work Armhole Edging

For the final inch before the armhole, work the stitches that correspond to the armhole depth in seed stitch to make a noncurling edging on the armhole. At the same time, work the 5 stitches immediately below the armhole in garter stitch to correspond to the garter edging at the hem edge (I worked 42 stitches in seed stitch along the armhole, 5 stitches in garter stitch right below the armhole, 42 stitches in stockinette stitch, and the last 5 stitches at the hem edge in garter stitch).

Bind Off for Armhole

Using the chain method (Glossary, page 131), bind off the armhole stitches (all of the stitches that were worked in seed stitch for the last inch) and leave the remaining stitches live for working the underarm panel.

Knit Underarm Panel

Work the remaining stitches in garter stitch until you reach the desired one-half bodice width. Because the row gauge for garter stitch is different from that for stockinette stitch, use the actual measurement of the piece instead of relying on your row gauge to determine when you've come to the right width.

Work Other Half of Back

Return the provisional stitches to your needle and remove the waste yarn to work the other half of the back in the opposite direction, matching the neck, armhole, and side panel. Double check that you have the same number of stitches as you cast on for the first half. If you are short a stitch, pick up an extra stitch into the second stitch at one side. If you have an extra stitch, work a decrease (k2tog or ssk) at the boundary between the garter-stitch edging and the stockinette-stitch body.

5 Determine Front Neckline Width and Depth

Using the bodice back as a guide, decide where you would like the base of the neckline to fall. The fronts will fold over from this point to the shoulder line, giving the appearance of a V neckline. The base of the V will mark the top of the center front overlap. I wanted the overlap to extend 13" above the hemline, which translated to the 56 stitches I cast on for the overlap.

6 Knit the Bodice Front

Knit the front in two pieces, each from the center front to the side seam. Working the left front first, use the long-tail method (Glossary, page 133) to cast on the desired number of stitches for the front overlap. Work the 5 stitches at the lower edge in garter stitch to match the lower back edging, and work the remaining stitches in seed stitch for 1³/₄" for the front overlap.

Cast On for Front Neck Depth

Use the long-tail method to cast on the number of stitches to bring you to the total desired bodice length. You should now have the same number of stitches as you cast on for the bodice back. Working the first and last 5

stitches in garter stitch as for the back, work the remaining stitches for the front edging in seed stitch for 1¹/₄". Work the next 2 rows substituting stockinette stitch for the seed stitch between the edgings (this helps the front neck edges to fold over). Knit the following two rows in garter stitch to create a garter ridge on the right side. Then work the rest of the bodice front to mirror the same side of the bodice back, ending by binding off stitches at the side seam edge of the underarm panel.

Determine Buttonhole Placement

In preparation for working the right front, determine where you want to position the button on the left front. Place your button at the desired point on the left front overlap—about ¹/₂" down from the top edge of the overlap and about ¹/₂" in from the cast-on edge is a good placement. Make note of the number of rows and stitches to the button placement so you can make a buttonhole on the right front to match. Knit a swatch if necessary to determine the right size buttonhole for your button (see Alina's Tip for Button Placement, page 59).

Knit the Right Front

Knit the right front as a mirror image of the left front, adding a buttonhole as desired.

7 Join Seams

Join the shoulder seams with a mattress stitch (Glossary, page 138). Join the side seams with a crochet chain stitch (Glossary, page 134) so that the seam allowance is on the right side of the garment.

8 Finishing Touches

Work as for the Side-to-Side Classic Crew (page 27). Sew button to left front opposite buttonhole.

Rose-to-Blue V-Necked Pullover

For this V-necked pullover, I varied the Side-to-Side Classic Crew by lengthening it and using a provisional cast-on at the center back and center fronts, and working each section outward to the cuff, ending with a narrow edging of seed stitch. At the neck and hemlines, I picked up stitches and knitted seed stitch for 1¹/₂". These changes, though minor overall, enabled me to gradate colors from cuff to cuff using a limited amount of handspun yarn.

Designer Notes

At the Black Sheep Wool Gathering in Eugene, Oregon, I bought the only 8-ounce bundle of Blue Faced Leicester fiber that Sandy had dyed in a beautiful rose and blue colorway. I later bought 4 ounces each of four beautiful colorways including predominantly geranium and cyclamen pink tones, and two with periwinkle and cobalt blues tones. When I laid them next to Sandy's roving, it looked as though I'd consciously chosen them to match. To get enough yarn for a sweater, I dyed 16 more ounces of roving in coordinating colorways for a total of 2¹/₂ pounds (so I'd have plenty to play with) of nine variegated rovings that grade from rose to blue.

I spun and plied the yarn in various combinations. I wound the yarn into balls and laid them in the sequence I envisioned for the sweater: from rose at one cuff through lavender to blue on the other. I chose the center color of the sequence for the center of the bodice. I rewound that ball into two balls of equal size and set aside one for the sweater front. I divided the other ball in two, one half for each side of the back. When that ball ran out, I chose the next yarn in the sequence and divided it into two balls (one for the front, one for the back) and continued in this fashion until I had completed one half of the sweater back. I set the remaining whole skeins in the sequence aside for that sleeve, then returned to the center line and began knitting my color sequence in the opposite direction, similarly dividing the balls as I worked to the other side seam. I set the remainder of the skeins in that sequence aside for that sleeve.

Once the back was knitted, I worked each front from the center to the side edges, maintaining the same color sequence as the back. For the center front, I wound off about a third of the yarn for the neckline edging before I divided the remainder in half. Once I got to the sleeves, I didn't have to divide the balls. I just knitted from shoulder to cuff using the color sequence I had already arranged for each side. I used a ball of yarn that had a good balance of all the colors for the hem edging. I worked the neckline edging with the ball I set aside from the center front.

I knitted the sweater from the center outwards so that I could manage the color sequence with the limited amount of yarn that I had. If the color sequence of the yarns weren't an issue, it would be easy to knit this sweater from one cuff to the shoulder, across the body to the other shoulder, then down to the other cuff.

$\mathcal{T}$he Fitter List for Rose-to-Blue V-Neck Pullover

Measure your body and allow for the appropriate amount of ease (see page 14) or measure a sweater that fits the way you like and enter the numbers below. Refer to your gauge swatch for your stitch and row gauges, then translate each measurement into numbers of stitches and/or rows as you go along.

Yarn

Yarn name: **My two-ply handspun**

Fiber content: **100% Blue Faced Leicester wool**

Weight classification: **Heavy worsted (between #4 Medium and #5 Bulky)**

WPI: **10**

Number of yards/pounds used: **1,214 yards; 23½ ounces**

Gauge

Bodice: Stitches per inch (in stockinette stitch): **4** Rows per inch: **6**

Needle size: **US size 9 (5.5 mm; 36" or longer circular)**

Details

Cast-on method: **Provisional**

Bind-off method: **Chain**

Selvedge treatment: **Chain stitch**

Sleeve increase/decrease method: **Paired decreases**

Seam technique: **Mattress stitch at shoulders and along sleeves; crochet chain stitch worked on the right side of the fabric (size H/8 [5mm] crochet hook) for side seams.**

Notes/Variations

V Neckline
Beginning at the center front (base of V), shape the V by casting on 3 stitches every 2 rows 10 times, then casting on 5 stitches once. Edge the neckline with 10 rows of seed stitch.

Sweater Measurements

Bodice

Circumference: **48** inches

Width (excluding overlaps): **24** inches; **144** rows

Cast-On Stitches (including selvedge stitches): **106** stitches

Length With Edging: **28** inches

Length Without Edging: **26½** inches; **106** stitches

Length of Lower Edging: **1½** inches; **10** rows

Armhole Depth: **10** inches; **40** stitches

Back Neck Width Without Edging: **7** inches; **42** rows

Back Neck Width With Edging: **5½** inches

Front Neck Depth Without Edging: **8¾** inches; **35** stitches

Front Neck Depth With Edging: **7¼** inches

Lower Front Neck Width: **NA**

Shoulder Width: **8½** inches; **52** rows

Sleeves

Sleeve Length Without Edging: **17** inches; **104** rows

Sleeve Length With Edging: **18** inches; **112** rows

Cuff Circumference: **9** inches; **36** stitches (includes 2 selvedge stitches)

Half Cuff Circumference: **4½** inches; **18** stitches

Cuff Length: **1** inches; **8** rows in seed stitch

Upper Arm Circumference: **20** inches; **80** stitches (plus 2 selvedge stitches)

Half Upper Arm Circumference: **10** inches; **40** stitches (plus 1 selvedge stitch)

Sleeve Taper Rate: **2 stitches decreased every 6 rows 3 times, then every 4 rows 20 times**

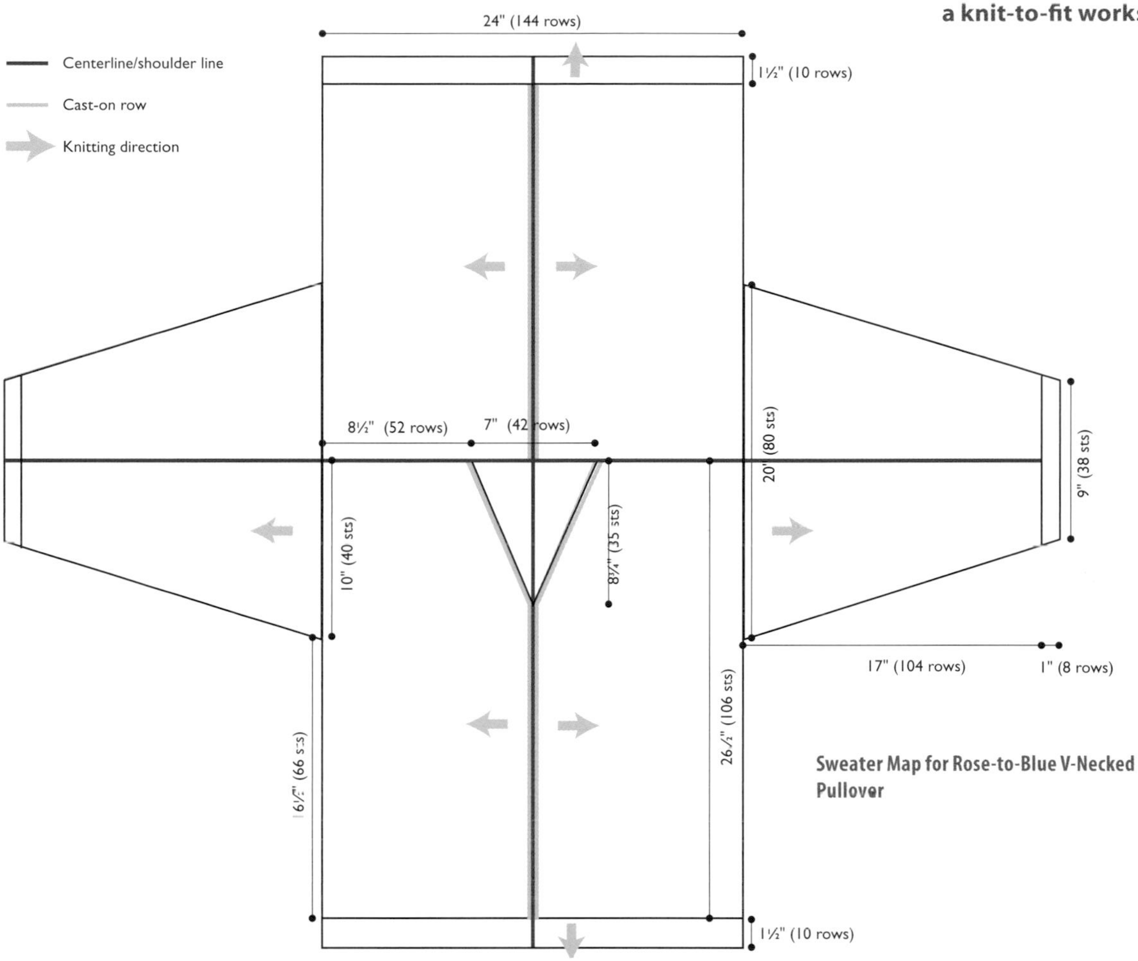

Centerline/shoulder line

Cast-on row

Knitting direction

24" (144 rows)

1½" (10 rows)

8½" (52 rows)   7" (42 rows)

20" (80 sts)

9" (38 sts)

10" (40 sts)

8¼" (35 sts)

17" (104 rows)   1" (8 rows)

26½" (106 sts)

16½" (66 sts)

1½" (10 rows)

Sweater Map for Rose-to-Blue V-Necked Pullover

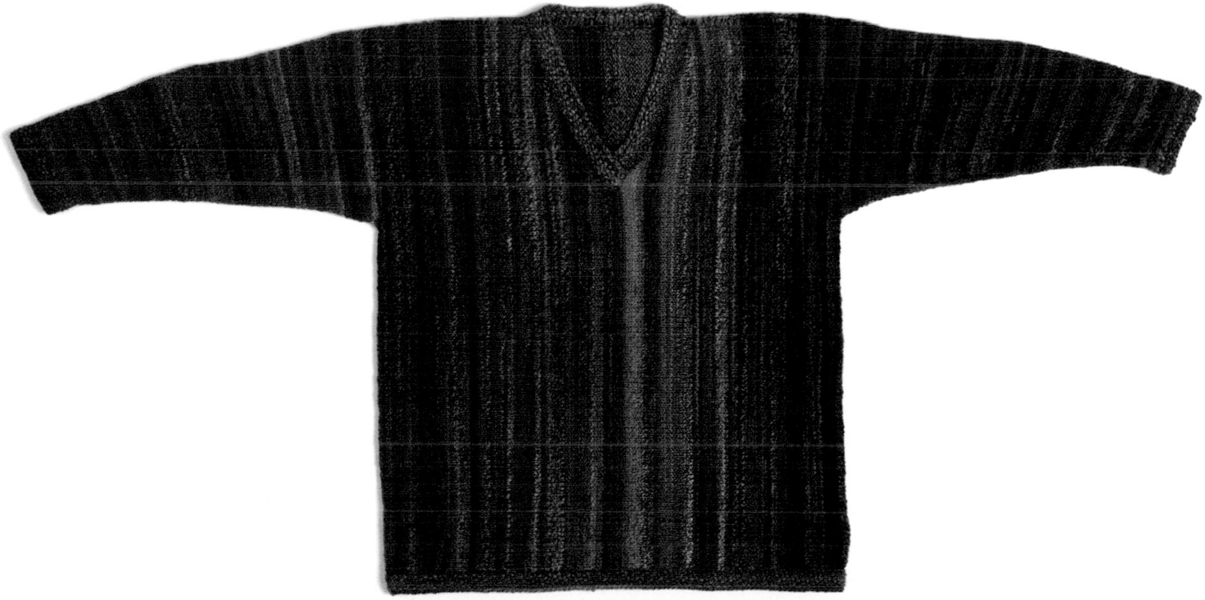

1 Determine Gauge

Work as for the Up-and-Down Classic Crew (page 17).

2 Determine Bodice Circumference and Length

Work as for the Up-and-Down Classic Crew (page 17).

3 Determine Stitch Count

Work as for the Side-to-Side Classic Crew (page 31).

4 Knit the Bodice Back

Work as for the Side-to-Side Classic Crew (page 31), but use a provisional cast-on (Glossary, page 134) at the center back and work each half to the side seam (for me, this was 72 rows), leaving stitches for the sleeves live (40 stitches in my case), and binding off the stitches between the lower edge and the base of the armhole (66 stitches in my case).

5 Determine Front Neckline Width and Depth

Work as for the Side-to-Side Classic Crew (page 32), but substitute a V neckline (page 39).

6 Knit the Bodice Front

Knit the front in two sections, beginning with a provisional cast-on at the center front and working each half outward to the side seam, shaping the V neckline along the way.

Determine Number of Stitches to Cast On

To determine the number of stitches to cast on for the front (71 stitches for me), subtract the number of stitches in the neckline depth without edging (35 stitches) from the total number of stitches cast on for the bodice back (106 stitches).

Shape V Neck

Following the neckline graph from center line outwards, shape the neckline by casting on stitches according to the taper rate of 3 stitches every 2 rows 10 times, then casting on 5 stitches once. When the neckline shaping is complete, there will be the same number of stitches as worked for the bodice back (106 stitches for me). Continue straight until the piece measures half the desired bodice width (12"), at which point you'll be at the side seam. Place the stitches that correspond to the half upper arm circumference (40 stitches) on waste yarn to work later for the sleeve. Use the chain method (see Glossary, page 131) to bind off the remaining stitches that correspond to the side seam (66 stitches). Remove the waste yarn from the provisional cast-on at the center front and work the other half of the front to match.

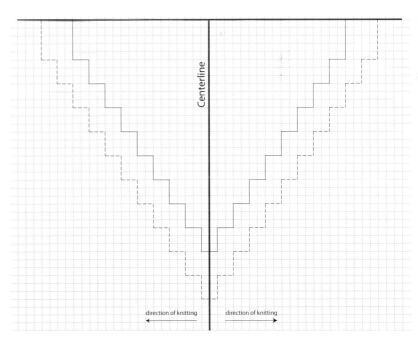

Neckline graph for Rose-to-Blue V-Necked Pullover

> ### Tip Hiding Chain Selvedges at the Shoulder Line
>
> When you knit the first row of the sleeve, work 2 stitches together on each side of the shoulder seam—use a left decrease (i.e., ssk; Glossary, page 135) on the right side of the seam and right decrease (i.e., k2tog; Glossary, page 135) on the left side. This will make the selvedge stitches disappear and eliminate an unsightly bump at the transition from shoulder to sleeve.

7 Determine Sleeve Dimensions

Work as for the Up-and-Down Classic Crew (page 22).

8 Determine Sleeve Taper

Work as for the Up-and-Down Classic Crew (page 24).

9 Knit the Sleeves

Join the shoulder seams and knit the sleeves from the shoulders to the cuffs, beginning with live stitches of the bodice front and bodice back.

Join the Shoulder Seams

Join the shoulder seams with a mattress stitch (Glossary, page 138).

Knit the Sleeves from Shoulder to Cuff

Return the number of stitches that correspond to the half upper arm circumference (40 stitches) for the bodice

My dyed fiber graded from dominantly rose to dominantly blue.

front and the bodice back to the needles. Work the sleeves downward to the cuffs, working paired decreases every 6 rows 3 times, then every 4 rows 20 times to end up with the desired number of stitches for the cuff (36 stitches). Work 8 rows of seed stitch for the cuff. Use the chain method to bind off all the stitches.

10 Join Seams

Join the side seams with a crochet chain stitch (Glossary, page 134) so that the seam allowance is on the right side of the garment. This is a decorative as well as a practical choice for heavy yarns that would otherwise make a bulky seam allowance on the inside of garment. Join sleeve seams with a mattress stitch (Glossary, page 138).

11 Add Edgings
Hemline

With a circular needle, pick up and knit about 3 stitches for every 4 rows around the hem. Work seed stitch in the round for 10 rounds. Use the chain method to loosely bind off all the stitches.

Neckline

Beginning at the base of the V, pick up and knit about 3 stitches for every 4 rows along the front neckline and about 1 stitch for every stitch across the back neck, then about 3 stitches for every 4 rows along the other front neckline. Work seed stitch for 1^1/$_2$". Use the chain method to bind off all the stitches. Overlap the edging at the bottom of the V and sew the selvedges of the edging band in place.

12 Finishing Touches

Work as for the Side-to-Side Classic Crew (page 35).

Sandy's Cardigan for Zylie

Sandy Sitzman designed this cardigan for her granddaughter Zylie. She followed the Side-to-Side Classic Crew, but began the bodice with a provisional cast-on at the center back. She worked each half sideways to the center front, with slits for the armholes made along the way (no side seams!). Sandy miscalculated the length of the armholes by ½" when she made her slits, so she improvised by adding 1" saddles across each shoulder. She then picked up stitches around the armholes and worked the sleeves in the round to the cuffs, tapering the sleeves on the fly. Sandy handdyed and handspun all the colors in this sweater, working intuitively to make it one of a kind. I knitted another alternative in yarns by Morehouse Farms to show how the pattern translates to handpainted yarns. The colors mentioned in the instructions are for this version, rather than Sandy's original.

Designer Notes

Any basic sweater pattern provides a blank canvas for all types of colorwork patterns. But how do you decide which patterns to use and where to put them? For Sandy, who believes in serendipity, this wasn't a problem. With a vision of how tall her granddaughter would probably be at the age of 4, she just started knitting with her joyful handspun, incorporating simple geometric pattern repeats. At any point she could decide to add a few rows to one side of the bodice and subtract from the other to center or shift the placement of her boldest patterns. As she approached the side seams, Sandy worked increasingly smaller patterns that required

fewer stitches and rows in the repeats. She patterned her bodice fronts to echo but not copy her bodice back, constantly changing the color combinations.

If you prefer to plan your design ahead of time, sketch your ideas on proportional knitter's graph paper (Resources, page 142) and color the shapes and motifs to represent your yarn colors. Knit a swatch of a representative portion of the color pattern to get an accurate gauge so you can calculate your stitch counts. When you know the exact number of stitches and rows in your sweater, you can draw the entire sweater on graph paper and color in the color pattern.

$\mathcal{T}$he Fitter List for Sandy's Cardigan for Zylie

Measure your body and allow for the appropriate amount of ease (see page 14) or measure a sweater that fits the way you like and enter the numbers below. Refer to your gauge swatch for your stitch and row gauges, then translate each measurement into numbers of stitches and/or rows as you go along.

Yarn

Yarn #1: **Sandy's handspun.**

Yarn #2: **Morehouse Merino Variegated 3-Strand (140 yards/2 ounces): Saffron and Indian Summer, 2 hanks each; Berry Patch, Fern Glen, Autumn Harvest, and Bordeaux, 1 hank each.**

Fiber content: **100% wool**

Weight classification: **Worsted (#4 Medium)**

WPI: **11**

Number of yards/pounds used: **12 ounces; 840 yards**

Gauge

Stitches per inch: **4.5 (in charted pattern)**

Rows per inch: **6 (in charted pattern)**

Needle size: **US 8 (5 mm) for bodice (straight) and sleeves (16" circular or set of double-pointed); US 6 (4 mm) for cuffs (set of double-pointed)**

Details

Cast-on method: **Long-tail**

Bind-off method: **Knit/Purl (K1, P1 Rib version) for collar and center front; chain for lower border and cuffs**

Selvedge treatment: **Stockinette stitch**

Sleeve increase/decrease method: **Paired decreases**

Seam technique: **NA**

Notes/Variations

Cardigan: Front Width Without Edging: 8^1/$_2$"; 51 rows
Center Front Overlap: 1"; 10 rows (added after lower border)
Six 1" buttons
Saddle Shoulders: Saddle Width: 12 rows garter stitch
Collar: Collar Length: 2^1/$_2$"; 18 rows

Sweater Measurements

Bodice

Circumference: **34** inches;

Width: **17** inches; **102** rows

Length With Edging: **19 (including shoulder saddle)** inches

Length Without Edging: **17** inches; **77** stitches

Length of Lower Edging: **1½** inches; **18** rows

Cast-On Stitches: **77** stitches

Armhole Depth: **6** inches; **27** stitches

Back Neck Width Without Edging: **8½** inches; **50** rows

Back Neck Width With Edging: **7½** inches

Front Neck Depth Without Edging: **2 (including half of shoulder saddle); 1½ inches; 7 stitches (without shoulder saddle)**

Front Neck Depth With Edging: **2** inches

Lower Front Neck Width: **1** inches

Shoulder Width: **4¼** inches; **26** rows

Sleeves

Sleeve Length Without Edging: **10** inches; **60** rounds

Sleeve Length With Edging: **12½** inches; **75** rounds

Cuff Circumference: **10 inches above edging; 8 inches below edging**

Half Cuff Circumference: **5 inches above edging; 4 inches below edging**

Cuff Length: **2½** inches; **15** rounds

Upper Arm Circumference: **12** inches; **54** stitches

Half Upper Arm Circumference: **6** inches; **27** stitches

Sleeve Taper Rate: **Beginning after 31 rounds, decrease 2 stitches every 7 rounds 4 times**

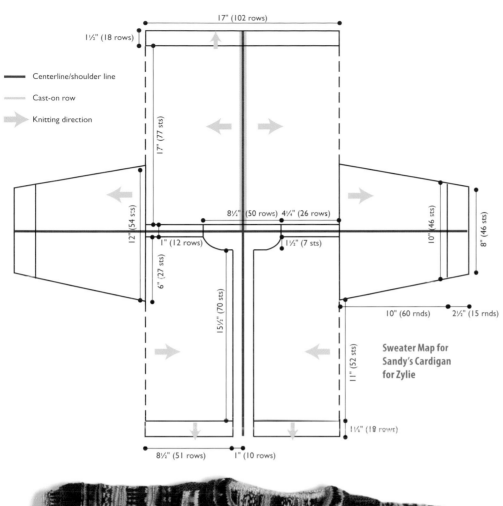

17" (102 rows)

1½" (18 rows)

Centerline/shoulder line

Cast-on row

Knitting direction

17" (77 sts)

12" (54 sts)

8½" (50 rows) 4¼" (26 rows)

10" (46 sts)

8" (46 sts)

1" (12 rows)

1½" (7 sts)

6" (27 sts)

15½" (70 sts)

10" (60 rnds) 2½" (15 rnds)

Sweater Map for Sandy's Cardigan for Zylie

1" (52 sts)

1¼" (19 rows)

8½" (51 rows) 1" (10 rows)

Commercial yarn

I knitted Sandy's sweater stitch for stitch in Morehouse Merino variegated yarns. I used one size larger needles, so the gauge is different and the sweater is slightly larger than Sandy's original. Handpainted yarns create a different effect than two-ply variegated handspuns, but the effect is still intoxicating.

Handspun yarn

Tip Sizing a Child's Sweater

For many of us, the sizing for children's sweaters is a mystery. To make an educated guess, refer to published patterns for sweaters that have a similar shape and use yarn of a similar weight. Or measure a ready-made sweater. You can also find helpful information on the Web—go to search engine such as Google and type in something like "children's armhole depths." You'll be surprised by the amount of information you can find this way.

Tip Changing the Size

To lengthen or shorten this sweater, simply add or subtract from Sandy's simple repeat patterns. To widen, more rows are necessary. To widen just a few rows, knit another stripe or two of a different color, or add an extra row of color between pattern repeats. To make this sweater substantially larger, choose your favorite pattern repeats and knit them again in different combinations or make up a few of your own.

Tip Provisional Cast-On with Color-Work Pattern

You can use a backward-loop cast-on as a provisional cast-on. Simply pick up every stitch in the cast-on row and knit in the opposite direction. Although this is not as invisible as a true provisional cast-on, it does not stagger the color-work pattern. You can disguise the juncture by working the first row after picking up stitches to make a garter ridge (knit on wrong side or purl on right side).

Left Front Bodice (not including edging)   **Left Back**   **Right Back**

☐ Knit on RS; purl on WS in color as shown

⊡ Purl on RS; knit on WS in color as shown

▢ Saffron

▢ Autumn Harvest

■ Indian Summer

■ Bordeaux

▢ Berry Patch

■ Fern Glen

☐ Pattern repeat

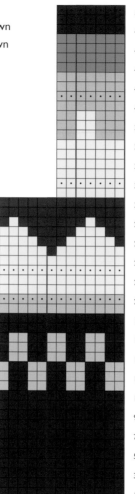

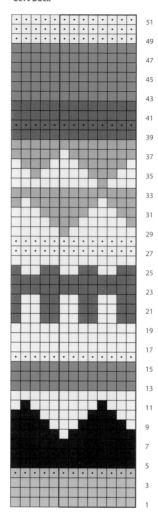

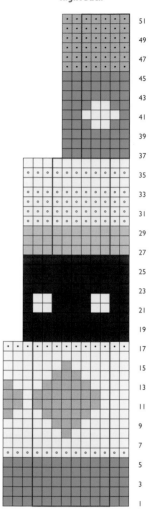

1 Determine Gauge

Work as for the Up-and-Down Classic Crew (page 17).

2 Determine Bodice Circumference and Length

Work as for the Up-and-Down Classic Crew (page 17).

3 Determine Stitch Count

Work as for the Side-to-Side Classic Crew (page 31).

4 Knit the Bodice Back

Work as for the Side-to-Side Classic Crew (page 31), but use a provisional cast-on (Glossary, page 134) at the center back and work each half to the side seam, following the charts for color pattern. Do NOT bind off the stitches.

Right Front Bodice
(not including edging)

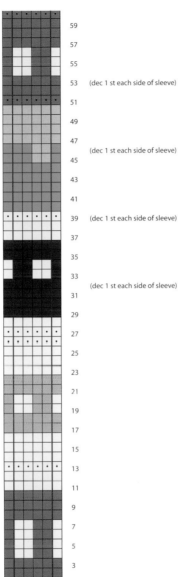

Left Sleeve
(without cuff)

59
57
55
53   (dec 1 st each side of sleeve)
51
49
47   (dec 1 st each side of sleeve)
45
43
41
39   (dec 1 st each side of sleeve)
37
35
33   (dec 1 st each side of sleeve)
31
29
27
25
23
21
19
17
15
13
11
9
7
5
3
1

Right Sleeve
(without cuff)

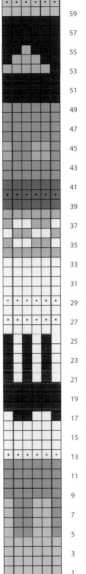

59
57
55
53   (dec 1 st each side of sleeve)
51
49
47   (dec 1 st each side of sleeve)
45
43
41
39   (dec 1 st each side of sleeve)
37
35
33   (dec 1 st each side of sleeve)
31
29
27
25
23
21
19
17
15
13
11
9
7
5
3
1

Lower Edging

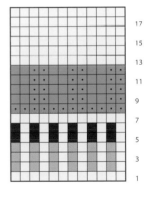

17
15
13
11
9
7
5
3
1

Left Center
Front Edging

9
7
5
3
1

Right Center Front Edging (with buttonholes)

9
7
5
3
1

Sleeve Cuffs

15
13
11
9
7
5
3
1

Collar

17
15
13
11
9
7
5
3
1

5 Determine Front Neckline Width and Depth

Work as for the Side-to-Side Classic Crew (page 32).

6 Knit the Bodice Front

Knit the fronts as continuations of the backs, working color pattern as charted and shaping the armholes and neckline as you go.

Shape Armholes

Shape the armhole by using the chain (or loop) method (Glossary, page 131–132) to bind off the number of stitches that corresponds to the armhole depth (for

Sandy's depth of 5½", she bound off 51 stitches). This forms the back edge of the armhole. On the next row, use the backward loop method (Glossary, page 133) to cast on the same number of stitches just bound off. This forms the front edge of the armhole.

Work to Center Front

Work each side separately to the center front, shaping the neckline according to the neckline chart. Work the fronts to about ½" short of the centerline (Sandy worked 4 rows short of the centerline) to accommodate the center front edgings. Place the stitches on waste yarn holders to work later for the edging.

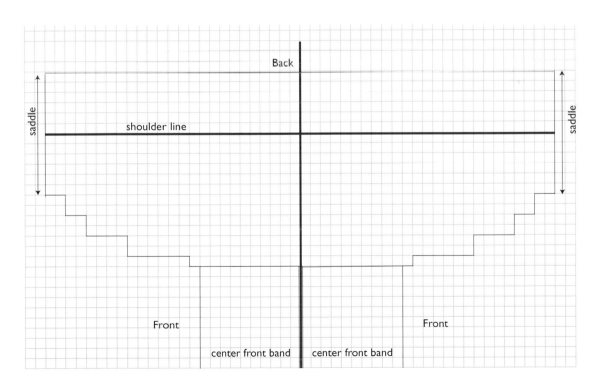

Neckline chart for Sandy's Cardigan for Zylie

7 Determine Sleeve Dimensions

Work as for the Up-and-Down Classic Crew (page 22).

8 Determine Sleeve Taper

Work as for the Up-and-Down Classic Crew (page 24).

9 Knit the Sleeves

Join the fronts and back with horizontal shoulder saddles, then pick up stitches around the armholes and knit the sleeves in the round from the shoulders to the cuffs.

Knit Shoulder Saddles

Pick up and knit 3 stitches for every 4 rows along the front shoulders. (This amounted to 20 stitches for Sandy.) Work in garter stitch for 1" (12 rows for Sandy), then bind off all the stitches. Use a mattress stitch (Glossary, page 138) to join the saddles to the back shoulders.

Knit the Sleeves from Shoulder to Cuff

With double-pointed needles or a short (16") circular needle, pick up and knit the number of stitches that corresponds to the upper arm circumference evenly spaced around the armhole (Sandy picked up 1 stitch for every stitch around the armhole and 1 stitch for every 2 rows in the saddle for a total of 54 stitches). Work the sleeves in the round to the cuff, following the charts on page 91 and at the same time, taper the sleeve as described in the Fitter List. Change to smaller needles as you work the cuff according to the chart on page 91. Use the chain method to bind off all the stitches.

10 Join Seams

There are no remaining seams to sew on this cardigan.

11 Add Edgings

Hemline

Pick up and knit stitches around the hemline at a rate of about 3 stitches for every 4 rows. Knit the bottom band according to the chart on page 91. Use the chain method to bind off all the stitches.

Front Bands

Return the left front stitches to the needle and pick up and knit stitches along the selvedge edge of the lower edging at a rate of 3 stitches for every 4 rows (Sandy had a total of 82 stitches). Knit the lower edging according to the chart on page 91. Decide on the placement of buttons (see Alina's Tip for Button Placement, page 59) and work the left front to match, working buttonholes to correspond to button placement. Use the knit/purl method for k1, p1 rib (Glossary, page 131) to bind off all the stitches.

Neckline

Pick up and knit stitches around the neckline at a rate of about 1 stitch for every stitch or 5 stitches for every 4 rows around the opening (Sandy had 108 stitches). Work k1, p1 rib for 3 rows, then center the Collar chart (on page 91), working the first 3 and last 3 stitches in garter stitch to prevent the edges from curling, then work 2 more rows of k1, p1 rib. Use the knit/purl method for k1, p1 rib to bind off all the stitches.

12 Finishing Touches

Work as for the Side-to-Side Classic Crew (page 35). Sew buttons to left front opposite buttonholes.

Gail's Red Aran

Gail Marracci used both up-and-down and side-to-side elements in this impressive Aran. She worked the bodice from the top down, but added side-to-side shoulder saddles that extended from the neck to the armholes, then continued down to the sleeve cuffs. Gail cast on for the neck, worked the neck in the round to the desired length, then separated the stitches for the bodice front, bodice back, and each shoulder saddle. She worked the saddles first for the length of the shoulders, then picked up stitches along the saddle selvedges and knitted the rest of the sweater from the top down, working the sleeves and the bodice below the armholes in the round. The bodice is worked in a combination of cable panels that make up the desired circumference.

Designer Notes

Gail had been working up to designing this Aran for 14 years, ever since she saw a red Penny Straker Aran Sweater in a yarn store window. She tried to find a red Aran on a trip to Scotland to no avail. When presented with the challenge to design a sweater, Gail didn't give it a second thought—it would be a red Aran.

"Since I had never designed my own Aran, I researched the nuts and bolts of constructing them in the traditional seamless top-down fashion. The hardest part was to select a limited number of cables. It was great fun to swatch all the cable patterns I liked and arrange them in a variety of ways. I modified the cable patterns to my preferences, then made my final decision based on how each cable looked next to its neighbors, being careful to choose cables with staggering row repeat numbers. Upon choosing the 'finalists,' I knitted a large swatch of the front including the whole center panel to confirm the overall cable interaction. I made my final calculations for size, the number of filler moss stitches required, and cast on."

The Fitter List for Gail's Red Aran

Yarn

Yarn name: **Chuckanut Bay Yarns: 100% Perendale Wool 10 ply (distributed by Russi Sales): #382 red, nine 390-yd hanks.**

Fiber content: **100% Perendale wool**

Weight classification: **(#4 Medium)**

WPI: **11**

Number of yards/pounds used: **3,200**

Gauge

Stitches per inch per panel:

Panel A, saddle: **8 (in charted pattern)**

Panel B: **5½ (in charted pattern)**

Panel C: **7 (in charted pattern)**

Panel D: **6½ (in charted pattern)**

Panel E: **5 (in moss stitch)**

Rows per inch: **7 (averaged for all stitches)**

Needle size: **US 8 (5 mm) for bodice and sleeves (36" circular); US 6 (4 mm) for edgings (16" circular or a set of double-pointed)**

Details

Cast-on method: **Loop**

Bind-off method: **Chain**

Selvedge treatment: **Stockinette stitch on saddle and upper bodice**

Sleeve increase/decrease method: **Paired decreases**

Seam technique: **NA**

Notes/Variations

Saddle Shoulders: *Front Neck Depth (Saddle Width):* 4"; 32 stitches
Length of Saddle (Shoulder Width): 10"; 70 rows
Sleeve Stitches Picked up Along Front Armhole: 30 stitches
Sleeve Stitches Picked up Along Back Armhole: 38 stitches
Collar: Length of Collar: 4" folds over to 2"; 29 rounds

Sweater Measurements

Bodice

Circumference: **50** inches

Width: **25** inches; **154** stitches

Panel A: **4** inches; **32** stitches

Panel B: **5** inches; **28** stitches (increases to 36 then decreases back to 28)

Panel C: **4** inches; **28** stitches

Panel D: **3** inches; **20** stitches (increases to 22 then decreases back to 20)

Panel E: **3** inches; **15** stitches

Cast-On Stitches: **120** stitches

Length With Edging: **27½** inches

Length Without Edging: **22** inches

Length of Lower Edging: **2½** inches; **18** rounds

Armhole Depth: **9** inches

Front Armhole Depth (not including saddle): **6** inches; **42** rows

Back Armhole Depth (not including saddle): **8** inches; **56** rows

Back Neck Width Without Edging: **5** inches; **28** stitches

Back Neck Width With Edging: **NA**

Front Neck Depth Without Edging: **4** inches; **32** stitches

Front Neck Depth With Edging: **2** inches

Lower Front Neck Width: **5** inches; **28** stitches

Begin Front Neck At: **NA**

Shoulder Width (Saddle Length): **10** inches; **70** rows

Sleeves

Sleeve Length Without Edging: **14** inches; **98** rounds

Sleeve Length With Edging: **16½** inches; **116** rounds

Cuff Circumference: **8** inches; **50** stitches

Half Cuff Circumference: **4** inches; **25** stitches

Cuff Length: **2½** inches; **18** rounds

Upper Arm Circumference: **18** inches; **100** stitches

Half Upper Arm Circumference: **9** inches; **50** stitches

Sleeve Taper Rate: **2 stitches decreased every 4 rounds 24 times, then work 2 rounds even, then decrease 2 stitches on last round**

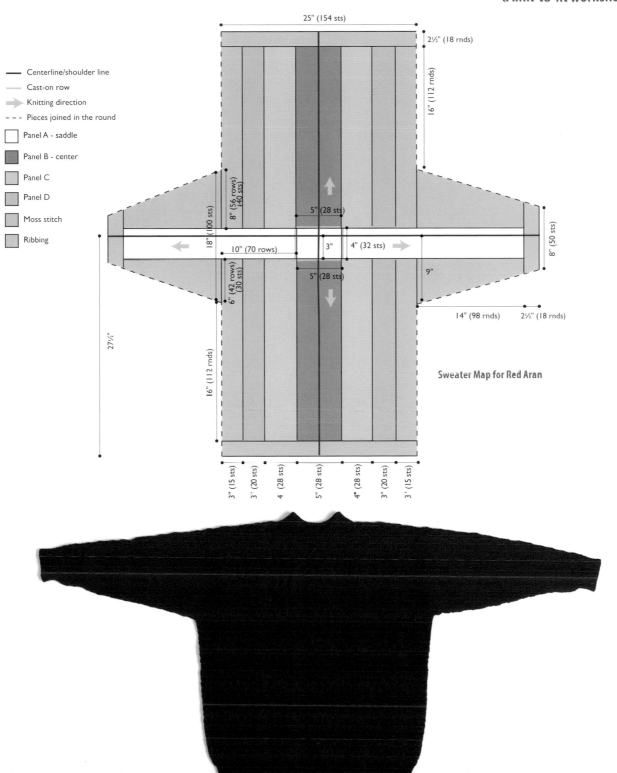

Centerline/shoulder line
Cast-on row
Knitting direction
Pieces joined in the round

Panel A - saddle
Panel B - center
Panel C
Panel D
Moss stitch
Ribbing

25" (154 sts)

2½" (18 rnds)

16" (112 rnds)

8" (56 rows) (40 sts)

5" (28 sts)

18" (100 sts)

10" (70 rows)

3"

4" (32 sts)

8" (50 sts)

5" (28 sts)

6" (42 rows) (30 sts)

9"

14" (98 rnds)   2½" (18 rnds)

27½"

16" (112 rnds)

Sweater Map for Red Aran

3" (15 sts)   3" (20 sts)   4 (28 sts)   5" (28 sts)   4" (28 sts)   3" (20 sts)   3" (15 sts)

1 Determine Gauge

Work as for the Up-and-Down Classic Crew (page 17), figuring the gauge for each panel separately.

2 Determine Bodice Circumference and Length

Work as for the Up-and-Down Classic Crew (page 17).

3 Determine Stitch Count

Determine the bodice stitch count based on the gauge of each panel. After swatching each panel, Gail moved them around to find the sequence she liked best, then she measured the collective width of the center five panels, which added up 19". Gail wanted a width of 25" so she needed to add another 6" in width. She added a 3"-wide panel of seed stitch to each side. Gail sketched the panels on her Sweater Map and added up the number of stitches in each to find the number of stitches she'd need in her bodice width.

4 Knit the Bodice Back and Front

The bodice back and front are worked from the top down, beginning with a faced mock turtleneck. When the neck is the desired length, stitches are divided for the back, front, and two shoulder saddles. The saddles are worked side to side to the length of the shoulder, then stitches are picked up along the selvedge edges of the saddles for the front and back, which are worked separately to the base of the armholes, and finally, the front and back are joined together and worked in the round to the hemline.

Determine Neckline Width and Depth

Using a ruler, measure the desired neck width and enter this number in the Fitter List. Using a tape measure, measure the desired front neck depth, which will be the same as the saddle width. Enter this number in the Fitter List.

Counting from your swatches, choose a cable panel for your center bodice that matches (or is close to matching) your desired neck width, and another panel that matches (or is close to matching) your desired neck depth. Refer to the box on page 102 for ways to add or subtract stitches to the panels if necessary to get the desired widths. Be sure to add a selvedge stitch at each edge of shoulder panels for picking up stitches for the front and back. Keep in mind that when working with cable patterns, it's not always possible to get exactly the number of stitches you aim for, but you can come close.

Tip **Determining Cable Arrangement**

Sample the cables in separate swatches so you can see how they work together.

Panel A (Saddle and Sleeve)

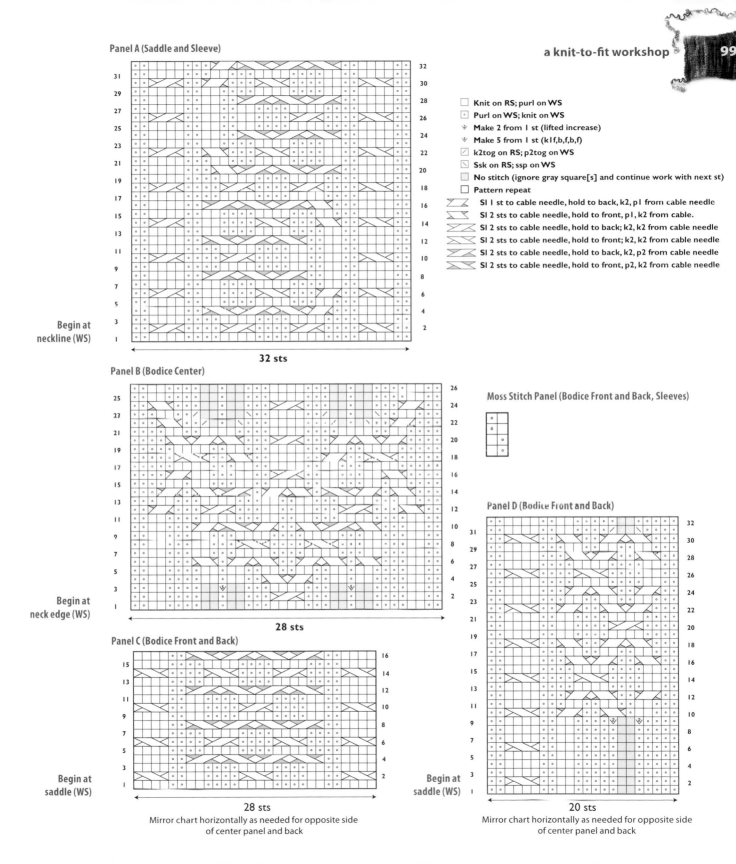

Begin at
neckline (WS)

32 sts

☐ Knit on RS; purl on WS
· Purl on WS; knit on WS
Ⅴ Make 2 from 1 st (lifted increase)
Ⅴ Make 5 from 1 st (k1f,b,f,b,f)
◺ k2tog on RS; p2tog on WS
◹ Ssk on RS; ssp on WS
☐ No stitch (ignore gray square[s] and continue work with next st)
☐ Pattern repeat
Sl 1 st to cable needle, hold to back, k2, p1 from cable needle
Sl 2 sts to cable needle, hold to front, p1, k2 from cable.
Sl 2 sts to cable needle, hold to back; k2, k2 from cable needle
Sl 2 sts to cable needle, hold to front; k2, k2 from cable needle
Sl 2 sts to cable needle, hold to back, k2, p2 from cable needle
Sl 2 sts to cable needle, hold to front, p2, k2 from cable needle

Panel B (Bodice Center)

Begin at
neck edge (WS)

28 sts

Moss Stitch Panel (Bodice Front and Back, Sleeves)

Panel D (Bodice Front and Back)

Panel C (Bodice Front and Back)

Begin at
saddle (WS)

28 sts

Mirror chart horizontally as needed for opposite side
of center panel and back

Begin at
saddle (WS)

20 sts

Mirror chart horizontally as needed for opposite side
of center panel and back

Determine Number of Stitches to Cast On

Determine the number of stitches to cast on for the mock turtleneck by adding the number of stitches in the center front panel (Panel B), the center back panel (Panel B), and the two shoulder saddle panels (Panel A). For Gail, this added up to 120 stitches.

Knit the Turtleneck

With smaller double-pointed needles or a short (16") circular needle, use the backward loop method (Glossary, page 133) to cast on stitches for the turtleneck and join for working in the round. Work in twisted rib until the piece measures 2", or the desired length of the facing. Purl all stitches on the next round to form a turning ridge. Continue in twisted rib until the piece measures 2" from turning ridge, or desired length.

Twisted K1, P1 Rib (even number of stitches)
All rows: *K1 through back loop, p1 through back loop; rep from *.

Divide for Bodice Front, Bodice Back, and Shoulder Saddles

Place the stitches for the bodice front on one holder, the stitches for one shoulder saddle on a second holder, and the stitches for the bodice back on a third holder, leaving the stitches for the remaining shoulder saddle on the needles. Gail put the first 28 stitches on one holder for the bodice front, the next 32 stitches on a second holder for one shoulder saddle, and the following 28 stitches on a third holder for the bodice back, leaving the remaining 32 saddle stitches on the needles. (There are more stitches on the saddles than the front or back due to the extreme draw-in of the shoulder cable panels.)

Knit the Saddles

Change to larger needle and work the saddle stitches according to Panel A chart (on page 99) for the desired shoulder width (Gail worked for 10"). Place these stitches on a holder. Return the stitches for the other saddle onto the needles and work them exactly the same way. Place these stitches on another holder.

Determine Neckline Depth and Saddle Width

Measure from a horizontal line parallel to the nape of your neck across your shoulder to a horizontal line parallel to the top of the notch of your sternum. Take the measurement directly beside your neck. It helps to have someone else take this measurement for you.

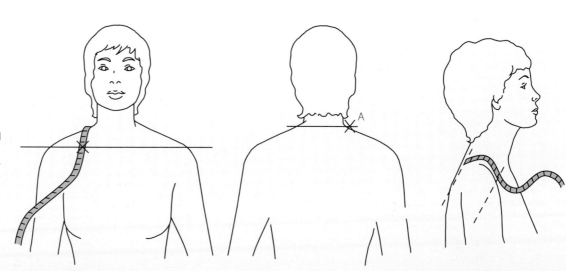

Knit the Bodice Back

With larger needles, pick up and knit the desired number of bodice stitches along the back selvedge edge of one saddle, knit across the held bodice stitches of the neckline, then pick up and knit the same number of stitches along the back selvedge edge of the other saddle. Gail picked up 63 stitches along each saddle and knitted 28 held stitches of the neckline for a total of 154 stitches. Work the stitches accord-

Adjusting Bodice Width with Cables

If you want to knit this sweater with a different finished width, you can adjust the number of stitches a variety of ways.

To Narrow or Widen a Little: The moss stitch panels at the sides of the central cable are the most easily adjusted. If you only need to adjust by a few stitches either side, start here. This is especially true if you want to widen the design.

To Narrow or Widen a Little More: If you want to narrow or widen the bodice dramatically, you can also remove or add purl stitches in the background border of each cable between the edges of the cables and the 4-stitch cables that separate each panel. For example, if you remove 1 purl stitch from each side of each of the five main cable panels, you'll remove a total of 10 stitches from the bodice width (20 stitches from the circumference). Conversely, if you add 1 stitch each side of those cable panels, you'll increase width by 10 stitches (and the circumference by 20 stitches).

You can also narrow the width by converting the 4-stitch cables to 2-stitch cables. This will result in 12 fewer stitches in the width (24 stitches fewer in the circumference). Widen the 4-stitch cables to 6-stitch cables, and you'll increase the width by 12 stitches (the circumference by 24 stitches).

To Narrow or Widen a Lot: Combine the above techniques for the most dramatic change. To convert Gail's sweater to a child's size, remove the smallest cable panel at both sides and leave the three central cable panels, or knit the sweater with a sportweight yarn on smaller needles, adjusting your stitch numbers accordingly.

ing to the cable panels until the piece measures the desired armhole depth. Gail worked 15 stitches according to the Moss Stitch chart, 20 stitches according to Panel D chart, 28 stitches according to Panel C chart, 28 stitches according to Panel B chart (center back), 28 stitches according to Panel C chart, 20 stitches according to Panel D chart, and the remaining 15 stitches according to the Moss Stitch chart.

Determine Armhole Depth

Because the shoulder saddles contribute to the armhole depth, the bodice back measured less than the total desired armhole depth. Gail wanted an armhole depth of 9". If she centered the 4" saddle along the shoulder line, 2" would contribute to the front armhole and 2" would contribute to the back armhole, and she'd need to knit the bodice for 7" to end up with the desired 9". But Gail wanted to shift the saddle forward 1" so that the saddle, which also accounts for the front neck depth, would be 3" deep on the bodice front and only 1" deep on the bodice back. This meant that Gail needed to knit the bodice back to 8" and the bodice front to 6" to end up with the desired 9" for each.

Knit the Bodice Front

With larger needles, pick up and knit stitches along the front selvedge edges of the saddles for the bodice front as for the bodice back. Work the front as for the back for 6" so that the total armhole depth is 9", as for the back (the saddles contribute 3" of the armhole depth on the front).

Join Bodice Back and Front

Join the stitches for the front and back and continue working the patterns as established in rounds until the bodice measures 2¹/₂" less than the desired length. Work in twisted rib on smaller needles as for the neck for 2¹/₂". Use the chain method (Glossary, page 131) to bind off all the stitches in pattern.

7 Determine Sleeve Dimensions

Work as for the Up-and-Down Classic Crew (page 22).

8 Determine Sleeve Taper

Work as for the Up-and-Down Classic Crew (page 24).

9 Knit the Sleeves

The sleeves are worked downward from the shoulders to the cuffs so that the held saddle stitches continue in the established cable pattern; the other stitches are picked up and worked in seed stitch.

Determine Number of Stitches to Pick Up

Using your moss stitch gauge as a guide, determine the number of stitches that corresponds to 6" along the front armhole (Gail picked up 30 stitches), and the number of stitches that corresponds to 8" along the back armhole (Gail picked up 38 stitches).

Pick up Stitches

Continuing in the established cable pattern, work across the saddle stitches, then pick up and knit the desired number of stitches evenly around the entire armhole, ending at the cable. On the next row, place a marker to

Cable Alignment

The cable panels in Gail's Aran are aligned vertically so that the center cable panel is centered at the center front (and center back) of the bodice. To align the cables vertically, the center stitch (or the space between the two center stitches) should fall along the bodice centerline. The cable panels on the bodice back are also aligned horizontally, that is, both Panel C and Panel D begin with the same row (Row 1) of the cable charts. However, because Gail chose to shift the shoulder saddles to the bodice front, the bodice front is shorter than the bodice back. Therefore, she began Row 1 of the charts lower on the bodice front than the bodice back. This simply means that when the front and back were joined at the base of the armholes for working in rounds, the pattern rows on the back did not match the pattern rows on the front.

If Gail had wanted to align the cables horizontally, she would have had to determine the difference in the number of rows in the bodice back and bodice front, and begin her back pattern that number of rows before the row she chose to start the front. Then, when she joined the two at the base of the armholes, she'd be at the same row of each pattern on the front and back.

mark the underarm seam line aligned at the bottom of the armhole. Work the sleeve in the round, working the taper rate as paired decreases on each side of the marker, ending 2¹/₂" short of the desired total length. Work twisted rib for 2¹/₂". Use the chain method to bind off all stitches.

10 Join Seams

Because the sweater was knitted in the round, there are no seams to sew.

11 Finishing Touches

Fold the collar to the wrong side of the work along the purled turning row and sew the facing to the inside. Weave in the loose ends. Lightly steam- or wet-block, being careful not to flatten the cables.

Angel Wing Lace Float

This feminine, flattering sweater in knitted in all directions. It begins with two center panels (one for the front and one for the back) that are knitted up and down as simple rectangles with no shaping. They're joined with single crochet along the selvedge edges from the hemline of the front panel to the hemline of the back panel, leaving a straight opening for the boat neck. Stitches are picked up along the crocheted edging and the side panels are worked side to side to the side "seams," then continue to the cuffs of the three-quarter-length sleeves. The armholes extend to the hemline, and the angel-wing sleeves taper along a gentle arc to the cuffs. A crocheted detail and a narrow shaped gusset are added along the side and sleeve "seams."

Designer Notes

I designed this sweater before I understood the need to compensate for differences in stitch and row gauge. I simply worked a chain stitch selvedge along the center panels to provide a loop every two rows that I could crochet into to provide a foundation for working the side panels. What seems like a mistake from a traditional point of view becomes a workable design element for any type of openwork or collapsible fabric. By slightly compacting the rows at the side seam, I caused the center panel to widen and curve gracefully at the neckline and at the hem.

Because the half-brioche stitch has a tendency to contract in length (especially when a crocheted edging is added) and also expand in width when it contracts, you may need to adjust stitch and row counts to maintain the basic shape measurements. If you find the center panel is compacting too much, change the size of the crochet hook or add or subtract stitches as necessary. Minor changes aren't difficult in this project, and the results are definitely worth the effort. But take the time to make a large swatch in half-brioche stitch and measure it before and after adding single crochet along the side edges to learn how much the piece will compact. Be prepared to factor in a few extra rows to get the length you want.

ℐhe Fitter List for Angel Wing Lace Float

Measure your body and allow for the appropriate amount of ease (see page 14) or measure a sweater that fits the way you like and enter the numbers below. Refer to your gauge swatch for your stitch and row gauges, then translate each measurement into numbers of stitches and/or rows as you go along.

Yarn

Yarn name: **Crystal Palace Country Silk. This discontinued yarn is a 2-ply sportweight silk noil.**

Fiber content: **100% silk noil**

Weight classification: **Sportweight (#2 Fine)**

WPI: **16**

Number of yards/pounds used: **1,130**

Gauge

Stitches per inch: **3½ for center panel (in half-brioche stitch) on smaller needles; 3⅓ for sleeves and side panel on larger needle (in garter stitch, stockinette stitch and half-brioche stitch)**

Rows per inch: **6¾ for center panel (in half-brioche stitch) on smaller needles; 6½ for sleeves (in half-brioche stitch) on larger needles; between 5 and 6½ for side panel (in garter stitch, stockinette stitch, and half-brioche stitch). Note: Work the number of rows you want in each pattern until the side panel is the desired width, adjusting stitch count if necessary to maintain length.**

Needle size: **US 10 (6 mm) for center panels (straight); US 10½ (6.5 mm) for side panels and sleeves (36" circular)**

Hook size: **E/4 (3.5 mm); change to larger hook if work compacts too much**

Details

Cast-on method: **Cable**

Bind-off method: **Chain**

Selvedge treatment: **Chain stitch**

Sleeve increase/decrease method: **Combination of bind-offs and paired decreases**

Seam technique: **Whipstitch**

Sweater Measurements

Bodice

Circumference: **48** inches

Width: **24** inches

Center Panel Width: **10** inches; **32** stitches

Side Panel: **5** inches; **28** rows

Cast-On Stitches: **32** stitches (center panel)

Length With Edging: **NA**

Side Panel Length Without Edging: **20** inches; **68** stitches

Center Panel Length Without Edging: **20** inches; **136** rows

Length of Lower Edging: **NA**

Armhole Depth: **20** inches; **68** stitches

Back Neck Width Without Edging: **10** inches; **32** stitches

Back Neck Width With Edging: **NA**

Front Neck Depth: **0** inches

Shoulder Width: **5** inches; **28** rows

Sleeves

Sleeve Length Without Edging: **12** inches; **78** rows

Sleeve Length With Edging: **NA**

Cuff Circumference: **10** inches; **32** stitches (not including gusset)

Half Cuff Circumference: **5** inches; **16** stitches (not including gusset)

Cuff Length: **NA**

Upper Arm Circumference: **40** inches; **136** stitches

Half Upper Arm Circumference: **20** inches; **68** stitches

Sleeve Taper Rate: **4 stitches bound off every row 6 times, then 2 stitches bound off every row 12 times, then 2 stitches decreased every 2 rows to cuff circumference**

Notes/Variations

Bodice worked in Sections
Width of Center Panel: 10"; 32 stitches
Width of Side Panel: 5"; 28 rows

Sleeve Gusset
Gusset Width At Hem: 2"; 10 rows
Gusset Width at Cuff: 1"; 5 rows
Gusset Length: 24"; 78 stitches

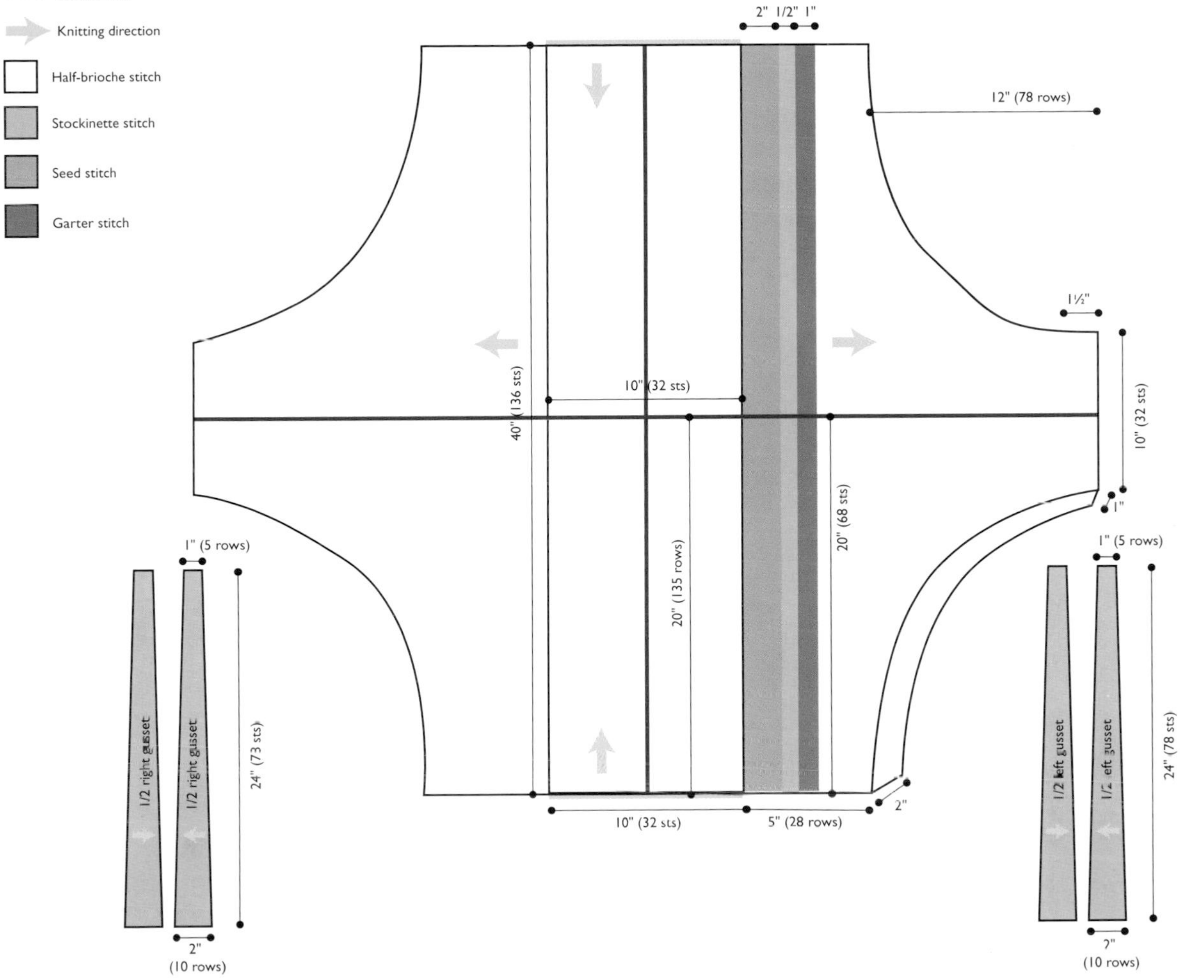

Centerline/shoulder line

Cast-on row

Knitting direction

Half-brioche stitch

Stockinette stitch

Seed stitch

Garter stitch

2" 1/2" 1"

12" (78 rows)

1½"

40" (136 sts)

10" (32 sts)

10" (32 sts)

1"

20" (135 rows)

20" (68 sts)

1" (5 rows)

1" (5 rows)

1/2 right gusset

1/2 right gusset

1/2 left gusset

1/2 left gusset

24" (73 sts)

24" (78 sts)

2" (10 rows)

2" (10 rows)

10" (32 sts)

5" (28 rows)

2"

Sweater Map for Angle Wing Lace Float

1 Determine Gauge

Work as for the Up-and-Down Classic Crew (page 17), working a swatch at least 6″ wide and 4″ long in half-brioche stitch, using the backward-loop cast-on and chain selvedges. Half-brioche stitch tends to expand widthwise and contract lengthwise (which lends the subtle shape to the sweater). Before measuring the gauge, loosely work 2 rows of single crochet along the selvedge edges at a rate of 1 stitch per selvedge chain. The crochet stitch will draw up the selvedge somewhat, but if you pull sideways on the crochet when you are finished, it will stretch back out. You want the crochet to compress the row gauge slightly, but not obviously. If your crochet draws the selvedge so noticeably that the fabric bunches, try working with a larger hook.

Half-Brioche Stitch (even number of stitches)
Set-up row: (WS) Purl.
Row 1: (RS) K1, knit into the stitch below the stitch on the needle, slip the stitch off the needle; repeat from *. (Caution: Don't make an increase by mistake; there should be no change in stitch count.)
Row 2: Purl.
Row 3: *Knit into the stitch below the stitch on the needle and slip the stitch off the needle, k1; repeat from *.
Row 4: Purl.
Repeat Rows 1–4 for pattern.

2 Determine Bodice Circumference and Length

Work as for the Up-and-Down Classic Crew (page 17), measuring your actual hip circumference (without any ease) for the bodice circumference.

3 Determine Stitch Count

The bodice front and back are each knitted in three panels. The center panel is worked up and down, and its width is determined by the desired boat neckline width.

Determine Center Panel Width

Using a ruler, measure the desired neck width, which will determine the center panel width. Multiply this width by your stitch gauge to determine the number of stitches to cast on for each center panel. I wanted my neckline to be about 10″ wide, so I cast on 32 stitches. Determine bodice length as for Up-and-Down Classic Crew (page 17).

Determine Side Panel Width

Subtract the width of the bodice center panel from the bodice width and divide this number in half to determine the width of each side panel.

4–9 Knit the Bodice Back, Bodice Front, and Sleeves

The bodice back and bodice front are identical. Both begin with a center panel that is worked up and down, then the two panels are joined along the selvedge edges with single crochet. Stitches are then picked up along each long crochet edge, and the side panels are worked side to side to the shoulders, then continue to the sleeve cuffs.

Knit the Center Panels

Using the cable method (Glossary, page 132), cast on stitches for the center panel. Using chain stitch selvedges (Glossary, page 139), work in seed stitch for 1″, then work in half-brioche stitch until the piece measures 1″ less than the desired total bodice length, using your row gauge as a guide for determining length. Work the final 1" in seed stitch, then use the chain method (Glossary, page 131) to bind off all the stitches. Keep in mind that when you work single crochet along the edges of the panel, the panel will become somewhat shorter and wider. Therefore, you may need to knit the panel 1" to 2" longer. Consult your gauge swatch to determine how much length is affected by the crochet. Make another piece to match.

Join Front and Back Center Panels

Position the front and back center panels so that the top rows of stitches are parallel. Beginning at the bottom right-hand corner of the front panel, work 1 single crochet stitch into each chain selvedge (1 stitch for every 2 rows of knitting). Continue along the side of the front panel to the top right hand corner, then continue along the back panel from the neck to the hemline. Turn the piece around and work a second row of single crochet on top of the first. When you're done, stretch the crochet stitches as necessary to straighten the edge. Repeat for the other selvedge edge of the panels, beginning at the back hemline and ending at the front hemline.

Knit the Side Panels

Using the larger-size circular needle, and working with the wrong side of the piece facing (so the line of crochet chains will show as a design element on the right side), pick up and knit 1 stitch in each crochet stitch from hemline to hemline. Work garter stitch for 2", stockinette stitch for ½", seed stitch for 1", then continue in half-brioche stitch to the

desired side panel width (including the 2 rows of crochet along the center panel). Leave the stitches live to continue in Step 9.

7 Determine Sleeve Dimensions

Place the stitches on several circular needles or waste yarn so that they can spread out to their full width. Slip the bodice over your head and determine the sleeve length as described for the Up-and-Down Classic Crew (page 23). You don't need to determine the armhole depth because the "wing" extends from the hemline to the cuff. Measure the length for a three-quarter-length sleeve. Determine the cuff circumference by measuring your arm where you want the three-quarter-length sleeve to end (the gusset will add 2" of ease to this circumference). My arm measured 10" in circumference at this point, which translated to 32 stitches.

8 Determine Sleeve Taper

Determine the taper as for the Up-and-Down Classic Crew (page 24), but instead of using the knitted fabric, draw the shape onto knitter's graph paper or make a full-sized template on Pellon yardage (page 46), and instead of drawing a straight line from the cuff to the base of the armhole, draw a gently curving line.

9 Knit the Sleeves

Knit the sleeves from shoulder to cuff as for the Up-and-Down Classic Crew (page 26), working in half-brioche stitch and following the desired taper rate. I shaped my sleeves by using the chain method to bind off 4 stitches at the beginning of the first 6 rows, then to bind off 2 stitches at the beginning of the next 12 rows. Then I worked paired decreases every other row until I reached

the number of stitches in my cuff circumference. I then continued straight until the sleeve measured the desired 17" from the pick-up row. Use the chain method to bind off all the stitches.

Knit the Gussets

The gussets are worked in two parts along each side/sleeve edge. The width can be adjusted, if desired, to add inches to or subtract inches from the bodice width. To prepare for picking up stitches along the side/sleeve edge, first work a row of single crochet (Glossary, page 134) around the entire edge of the sweater, working stitch for stitch along the bodice edge, 2 stitches into the corner stitch at the hem/sleeve junction, stitch for stitch into the front half of the bind-off loops along the bottom portion of the sleeve taper, 1 stitch for every 2 rows along the sleeve selvedge (work into the front half of the selvedge chain), and stitch for stitch along the cuff. Turn the work around and work another row of single crochet, working stitch for stitch in the previous row.

With the larger knitting needle, pick up and knit 1 stitch from the back half of every stitch in the first row of crochet along the side/sleeve edge (I picked up 78 stitches) so that the 2 rows of crochet form a decorative

---

Tip **Adjusting Gusset Shape**

You can adjust the shape of the gusset by increasing or decreasing the number of short-rows. For example, if you want each side of the gusset to be 4" wide at the hemline and 1" wide at the cuff, work fewer stitches between short-row turns and work more short-rows to increase the overall number of rows at the hemline edge.

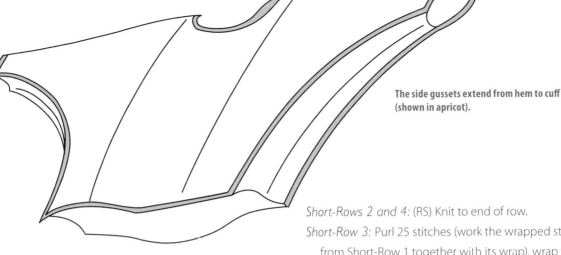

The side gussets extend from hem to cuff (shown in apricot).

edge that stands out from the knitting. Work 2 rows in stockinette stitch. Work short-rows (Glossary, page 140) in stockinette stitch so that the gusset is 1" wide at the cuff edge and 2" wide at the hem edge. I worked three sets of short-rows as follows:

Short-Row 1: (RS) Knit 15 stitches, wrap the next stitch, turn work.

Short-Rows 2 and 4: (WS) Purl to end of row.

Short-Row 3: Knit 25 stitches (work the wrapped stitch from Short-Row 1 together with its wrap), wrap the next stitch, turn work.

Short-Row 5: Knit 42 stitches (work the wrapped stitch from Short-Row 3 together with its wrap), wrap the next stitch, turn work.

Short-Row 6: Purl to end of row.

Work 2 rows in stockinette stitch, working the wrapped stitch from Short-Row 5 together with its wrap when you come to it. Bind off all the stitches.

Reverse the shaping for second half of the gusset as follows:

Work 3 rows in stockinette stitch (ending at hemline edge).

Short-Row 1: (WS) Purl 15 stitches, wrap the next stitch, turn work.

Short-Rows 2 and 4: (RS) Knit to end of row.

Short-Row 3: Purl 25 stitches (work the wrapped stitch from Short-Row 1 together with its wrap), wrap the next stitch, turn work.

Short-Row 5: Purl 42 stitches (work the wrapped stitch from Short-Row 3 together with its wrap), wrap the next stitch, turn work.

Short-Row 6: Knit to end of row.

Work 3 rows in stockinette stitch, working last wrapped stitch together with its wrap when you come to it. Use the chain method to bind off all the stitches.

Join the two gusset halves with a whipstitch (Glossary, page 139) through one-half of the bind-off loops so that the bind-off stitches lie flat for a decorative seam.

10 Join Seams

This seam lies where the two halves of the gusset meet under the arms. For a decorative seam, place the two bind-off edges side by side and join with a whipstitch.

11 Add Edgings

Work 2 rows of single crochet around the neck opening, working 1 crochet stitch in each stitch around the neck opening.

12 Finishing Touches

Work as for the Side-to-Side Classic Crew (page 27).

Laurie's Panel Jacket

This colorful jacket shows how far you can go with the Knitter Fitter system. Laurie Weinsoft sketched a Sweater Map, then she divided the sweater pieces into panels to be worked in different yarns, different stitch patterns, and different directions. The panels for the bodice fronts and back are worked up and down; the sleeves are worked side to side. Laurie modified the modified drop shoulder shaping by extending the front half of the sleeve caps nearly to the neckline. She modified the V neckline by adding shaped tabs to accommodate a pin closure so she didn't need to add a buttonhole.

The bodice back consists of three separate panels worked up and down from hemline to neckline and sewn together with mattress-stitch seams. The bodice front is split into two halves, each worked in two panels—a center panel and a side panel—upward from the hemline. The front half of the upper sleeve is worked side to side starting with stitches picked up along the center front panels and worked outward to the side seam, then stitches are picked up along the armhole depth of the back, and the sleeves are worked in a diagonal intarsia color pattern to the cuffs.

Designer Notes

"I really love wild colors, mixing stripes, and almost any type of pattern. I do dress this way, with lots of colors going every which way. I tell my students about how one day at the mall my husband turned to me and whispered that people kept touching me and pointing at me. I laughed and said it happens all the time. After all it isn't often that people find a large-size lady dressed in such flashy styles and touchable fibers."

As to size and yarn choice, Laurie says, "This is a very dramatic sweater. It could easily be worked in a single color, shorter length, or much smaller size. The thing I really like about panel work is that I can use my smaller amounts of handspun. The combination of commercial yarn and handspun can be a wonderful marriage. Try it, you'll love it!"

Laurie used her handspun curly mohair yarn for the front center bodice panels and front shoulder panels. She tends to spin very fine yarn and is accustomed to doubling it to make a thicker yarn, often blending two colors together. Because of the yarn mixtures, Laurie's gauge differed a little with each panel; she changed needle size when necessary to maintain consistent gauge.

$\mathcal{T}$he Fitter List for Laurie's Panel Jacket

Yarn

Yarn #1: __Berroco Optic: #4950 Montmartre, 16 balls (about 1390 yards)__

Fiber content: __48% cotton, 21% acrylic, 20% mohair, 8% metallic, 3% polyester__

Weight classification: __Worsted (#4 Medium)__

WPI: __11 (with yarn doubled)__

Yarn #2: __Laurie's handspun mohair, about 2,000 yards total of 4 colors (used double)__

Fiber content: __100% kid mohair, spun from locks (which makes a curly yarn)__

Weight classification: __Sportweight (#2 Fine) when single; worsted (#4 Medium) when doubled__

WPI: __11 (with yarn doubled)__

Number of yards/pounds used: __1,390 yards of Berroco Optic (Yarn #1); 2,000 yards of handspun (Yarn #2)__

Gauge

Stitches per inch: __3 (in reverse stockinette stitch)__

Rows per inch: __4½ (in reverse stockinette stitch)__

Needle size: __US 10 (6 mm) for panels; US 8 (5 mm) for cuffs;__

Hook size: __J/10 (6 mm)__

Details

Cast-on method: __Long-tail__

Bind-off method: __Chain__

Selvedge treatment: __Chain stitch__

Sleeve increase/decrease method: __Paired decreases__

Seam technique: __Mattress stitch__

Sweater Measurements

Bodice

Circumference: __76__ inches

Width: __38__ inches

Cast-On Stitches: __Depends on desired panel width__

Length With Edging: __NA__

Length Without Edging: __33__ inches; __148__ rows

Length of Lower Edging: __NA__

Armhole Depth: __12__ inches; __54__ rows

Back Neck Width Without Edging: __10__ inches

Back Neck Width With Edging: __10__ inches; __29__ stitches __44__ rows

Front Neck Depth Without Edging: __NA__

Front Neck Depth With Edging: __7__ inches; __32__ rows

Begin Front Neck At: __116__ rows

Shoulder Width: __11½__ inches; __36__ rows

Sleeves

Sleeve Length Without Edging: __15__ inches; __68__ rows

Sleeve Length With Edging: __16__ inches

Cuff Circumference Above Edging: __12__ inches; __36__ stitches

Cuff Circumference With Edging: __8__ inches; __36__ stitches

Half Cuff Circumference: __6__ inches; __18__ stitches (not including gusset)

Cuff Length: __1__ inches; __6__ rows

Upper Arm Circumference: __40__ inches; __136__ stitches

Half Upper Arm Circumference: __24__ inches; __72__ stitches

Sleeve Taper Rate: __2 stitches decreased every 2 rows to desired cuff circumference__

Notes/Variations

Cardigan

Center Front Overlap: 4" (at hem); 14 stitches

Front Top Side Panels: 36 stitches; 36 rows

Front Bottom Side Panels: 94 rows

Begin Shaping Tab on Center Front After: 58 rows

Width of Front Centerline Border: 7 stitches

Back worked in Panels

Center Back Panel Width: 15"; 45 stitches

Side Panel Width: 11½"; 35 stitches

Front Worked in panels

Center Front Panel Width: 9½"; 23 stitches

Side Panel Width: 11½"; 35 stitches

Modified Drop Shoulders

Across-Front Width: 15"

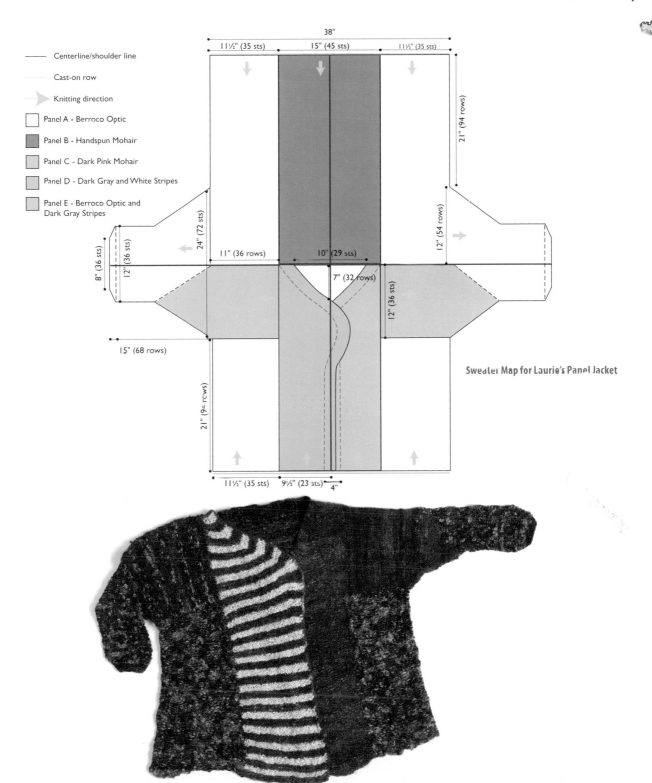

Centerline/shoulder line

Cast-on row

Knitting direction

Panel A - Berroco Optic

Panel B - Handspun Mohair

Panel C - Dark Pink Mohair

Panel D - Dark Gray and White Stripes

Panel E - Berroco Optic and Dark Gray Stripes

38"

11½" (35 sts)   15" (45 sts)   11½" (35 sts)

21" (94 rows)

24" (72 sts)

12" (36 sts)

8" (36 sts)

12" (54 rows)

11" (36 rows)   10" (29 sts)

7" (32 rows)

12" (36 sts)

15" (68 rows)

21" (94 rows)

Sweater Map for Laurie's Panel Jacket

11½" (35 sts)   9½" (23 sts)   4"

> ## *Tip* <u>Accounting for Stretch</u>
> Whether combining 2 or 20 yarns in a project, it isn't always possible to predict how much a sweater will stretch when worn. No matter how hard you may try to knit to exact specifications, the knitted fabric often has a mind of its own. The heavier the yarn, the larger the sweater, and the larger the needle size, the more possibility there is for the fabric to stretch during wear. Stitch patterns also can amplify or restrict stretch. Body heat and humidity affect stretch. To account for the stretch before knitting a sweater that grows too long, knit an ample swatch with a stretchy cast-on and bind-off. If the yarns are washable, wash the swatch. Carry it around, hang it on a doorknob, stretch it, tug it, and generally give it the run-around. Then measure it for gauge.

1 Determine Gauge

Work as for the Up-and-Down Classic Crew (page 17), working with a single strand of Berroco Optic or a double strand of handspun mohair.

2 Determine Bodice Circumference and Length

Work as for the Up-and-Down Classic Crew (page 17).

3 Determine Stitch Count

Figure the stitch count for each panel based on the desired panel width. Laurie wanted the center back panel

to be 15" wide, so for her gauge of 3 stitches per inch, she cast on 45 stitches. She figured the stitch counts for the other panels in the same way.

4 Knit the Bodice Back

Knit the bodice back in three separate panels.

Center Panel

Using the long-tail method (Glossary, page 133), cast on stitches for the desired width, work even to the shoulder line, then use the chain method (Glossary, page 131) to bind off all the stitches. Laurie cast on 45 stitches with two strands of her finely spun mohair held together and worked in reverse stockinette stitch for 33".

Side Panels

Make two side panels the same—cast on stitches for the desired width, work even to the shoulder, then bind off all the stitches. For each side panel, Laurie cast on 35 stitches with Berroco Optic and worked in reverse stockinette stitch for 33".

Join Back Panels

Using a mattress stitch (Glossary, page 138) and beginning at the hemline edge, sew one side panel to each selvedge edge of the center panel.

5 Determine Front Neckline Width and Depth

Determine the front neckline width by counting in 8 stitches from the sides of the center back panel. Of these stitches, 7 will become the center front border and 1 will be the selvedge stitch you'll use for picking up stitches or for seaming later.

The base of the neck opening occurs at the point where the bodice fronts cross at the centerline. The shaped tab will extend several inches beyond the center front. Whether you make your center front panels wide enough for a double-breasted style or design them to meet at the centerline with no overlap (Laurie split the difference with a 4" overlap), the taper rate will work the same. As long as the combination of the two overlapped center panels are as wide as the across-front measurement, the neckline should be centered and fall into proportion no matter what size you make the rest of the jacket.

Graph the Neckline

Center the number of stitches in your center back panel along the shoulder line of the neckline graph. Mark 1 stitch inside the selvedge on each side; these stitches will be the side selvedge stitches of the center front panel. Count and mark 7 stitches to the inside of each selvedge stitch for the center front borders. The stitches between the marks represent the front borders. The innermost stitch of the 7 marks the boundary of the neck width. Draw a taper line beginning just inside the selvedge stitch at the rate of 1 stitch every 2 rows until you reach the center front line, which will determine the front neck depth. Laurie reached the centerline after 32 rows, which translated to a depth of 7".

Next, decide how much you want the center front panels to overlap at the tab (Laurie wanted 7 stitches of overlap, plus 7 stitches for the front border). Extend the neckline taper to this point. The more overlap you choose, the lower the tab will ride on the bodice front and the longer the taper line of the neckline shaping. To complete the tab, draw a vertical line down 4 rows, then reverse the neckline taper.

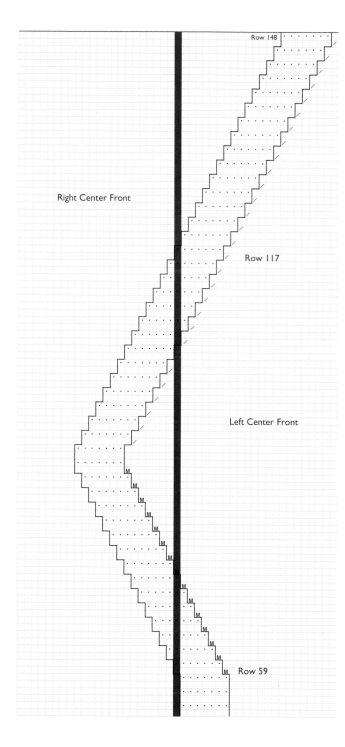

Right Center Front

Row 148

Row 117

Left Center Front

Row 59

Now draw a line from the shoulder line to the hemline that parallels the taper line but is 7 stitches away. These 7 stitches will be worked in the edging stitch (Laurie chose garter stitch). Add symbols to the graph to indicate increases and decreases necessary to shape the neckline taper, and to indicate the garter stitch pattern of the edging stitches. Double-check that you're happy with the neckline depth by marking the depth on the center stitch of the center back panel. If you want a shallower neck depth, the easiest way is to make the neck width narrower, leaving a larger number of stitches along the shoulder line of your graph. If you want a deeper neck depth, you'll need to change your taper rate.

Extend the neckline graph all the way to the hemline (you may need to tape together several pieces of graph paper to do this or indicate the row number where your chart begins). Label the row where you want to begin the tab and the row where you want to begin the V shaping. Follow the chart for the center front panels.

M   Inc 1 st using backward loop CO

⟋   K2tog

·   Purl on RS; knit on WS

—   Centerline/shoulder line

Neckline chart for Laurie's Panel Jacket. Shaded squares indicate the center front. Increases and decreases are worked 7 stitches from the center front. Those 7 stitches are worked in garter stitch for the front edgings.

Tip **Drawing the Neckline Graph**
If you have a flatbed scanner, draw just one side of the neckline graph, scan the graph, and reverse the image horizontally for the mirror image. Alternatively, take the graph to a copy shop and ask to have it done for you.

6 Knit the Bodice Front

The fronts are worked in two halves—the left front and the right front (as worn). Each half is worked in two separate panels, a center front panel and a side panel, each worked upward from the hemline.

Left Center Front Panel

With the desired color, cast on the number of stitches that corresponds to the desired center front panel width (Laurie cast on 23 stitches with dark pink mohair). On right-side rows, purl the first 16 stitches and knit the last 7 stitches (use a marker at the boundary, if desired). On wrong-side rows, purl all stitches. Continue in the manner until the piece measures the desired length to the base of the overlap tab. Follow the neckline graph to shape the tab and V neck to the shoulder line. Place the stitches on a holder.

Right Center Front Panel

With the desired color, cast on the number of stitches that corresponds to the desired center front panel width (Laurie cast on 23 stitches with dark gray mohair). On right-side rows, knit the first 7 stitches as usual and work the remaining 16 in striped garter stitch. On wrong-side rows, knit all stitches in the established colors. Continue in this manner to mirror the left center panel, alternating 4 rows of dark gray with 4 rows of natural white, until the piece measures the desired length to the base of the

tab. Follow the neckline graph to the shape the tab and V neck to the shoulder line (Laurie was left with 8 stitches at the shoulder). With the same yarn used for the center back panel and right side facing, knit across the remaining stitches of the right center front panel. On the next row, bind off all but the 7 stitches of the garter edging (Laurie bound off just 1 stitch; if you adjusted for a shallower neckline, you will have to bind off more stitches). Knit the 7 remaining stitches in garter stitch for the back neck edging to the length that corresponds to back neckline width. Place the stitches on a holder.

Striped Garter Stitch (worked on right center front panel)
Rows 1 and 2: Knit.
Row 3: Purl.
Row 4: Knit.
Repeat Rows 1–4, changing colors on Row 1 of each repeat.

Join Fronts to Back at Neckline

With the same yarn as used for the center back panel, knit across the remaining stitches of the left center front panel. On the next row, bind off all but the 7 stitches of the garter edging. Use the Kitchener stitch (see Glossary, page 136) to join the 7 garter edging stitches of the back neck edging to the remaining 7 stitches of the left center front panel. Use a mattress stitch to sew the neck edging to the top of the back center panel.

Determine Armhole Depth and Length of Side Front Panels

Try on joined the joined bodice to determine the armhole depth. The sleeve caps will extend across the fronts to the center panels, in an exaggerated modified drop shoulder shaping (see page 40). The Side Front Panels will end at the base of the armholes. Laurie made her armhole a generous 12" deep to match the oversized proportions in the rest of the garment.

Knit the Front Side Panels

Make two side panels the same—cast on stitches for the desired width, work even to the base of the armhole, then bind off all the stitches. For each side panel, Laurie cast on 35 stitches with Berroco Optic and worked in reverse stockinette stitch for 21".

Join Front Panels

Using mattress stitch and beginning at the hemline edge, sew one side panel to the straight selvedge edge of each center panel.

Knit the Front Shoulder/Sleeve Panels

With the desired color, pick up and knit stitches along the selvedge edge of the center front panel at a rate of 3 stitches for every 4 rows from the base of the armhole to the shoulder line (Laurie picked up 36 stitches, using dark pink mohair for the left front and dark gray mohair for the right front). Work in the desired stitch pattern until the panel extends across the full width of the front side panel. (Laurie worked for 11½", working the left front in reverse stockinette stitch and the right front in garter stitch, alternating uneven stripes of dark gray mohair and Berroco Optic.) Place the stitches on holders. Use a mattress stitch to sew the lower edge of the shoulder/sleeve panel to the top of the side panels.

7 Determine Sleeve Dimensions

Work as for the Up-and-Down Classic Crew (page 22), using the number of live shoulder/sleeve panel stitches for the half upper arm circumference.

8 Determine Sleeve Taper

Work as for the Up-and-Down Classic Crew (page 24), or do as Laurie did and simply work paired decreases every other row until you have the number of stitches that corresponds to the desired cuff circumference.

9 Knit the Sleeves

Work across the live stitches of the shoulder/sleeve panel on the front, then pick up and knit the same number of stitches along the back side panel between the shoulder line and armhole depth. Knit the sleeves in the desired

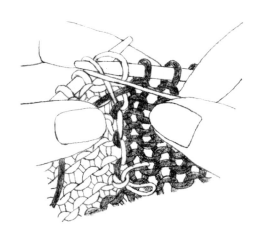

When changing from one color to the next in intarsia color work, be sure to cross the two yarns around each other on the wrong side of the work to prevent holes from forming at the color changes.

color from shoulder to cuff, following the desired taper. (Laurie worked a diagonal intarsia color change about halfway down each sleeve, changing one stitch per row from dark pink mohair in reverse stockinette stitch to Berroco Optic in garter stitch for the left sleeve and changing from stripes of Berroco Optic and natural dark gray to all Berroco Optic on the right sleeve. She worked paired decreases every other row along the way until she had 36 stitches for her cuff circumference.) Continue working straight until you reach the desired sleeve length without edging. Change to needles two sizes smaller (to draw in the cuff without decreasing stitches) and work in garter stitch for 1". Use the chain method to bind off all the stitches.

10 Join Seams

Use a mattress stitch to sew the side and underarm seams.

11 Add Edgings

Work a row of single crochet along the center front edges, matching the colors of the center panels. (Laurie used dark pink on the left front and dark gray on the right front.)

12 Finishing Touches

Weave in loose ends. Sew decorative bottons to the center back panel, if desired.

A Twisted Sisters Gallery of Inspiration

Four Corners

Lori and I collaborated to design, dye, spin, and knit this sweater for a competition. We split the work and met once a week to coordinate our progress (luckily we only lived an hour apart at the time). We made a Pellon template similar to the shape of Lori's Jacob's Windows (page 68), but with a V neckline. We cut the template into panels and sleeves and knitted each piece separately. The template was essential for coordinating our measurements because our stitch gauge was the same but our row gauge was not. I knitted my panels in intarsia; Lori knitted in stranded color work. For added interest, we knitted the panels perpendicular to each other. Because of the slight differences in our knitting, it required patience and focus to join the panels with a combination of Kitchener and mattress stitches. The neckline, hem and cuffs are edged with narrow bands of seed stitch.

Between the two of us, we dyed more than 25 different colorways of roving in blends of merino with silk, cashmere, alpaca, and angora, not to mention a couple of preciously hoarded naturally dyed blends from Copper Moth. We split every roving down the middle and swapped so that we each spun with every roving. We plied these colorways in countless combinations, coming up with at least 70 different yarns (but who's counting?).

Friendship Sweater

Lori and I each worked half of this side-to-side cardigan. It's similar to Sandy's Cardigan for Zylie (page 87), but with a V neck and asymmetrical triangular edgings. We lived 2,000 miles apart and worked without seeing the other's half. Even though our row gauges were slightly different, we were able to match the sizes by using a Pellon template. This is a sister sweater to Four Corners.

Lori and I began designing with two red family colorways of merino wool/tussah silk roving. Over two months of intensive dyeing, spinning and knitting, we came up with 9 colorways that ran the gamut of autumn warm tones plus black. We even matched each others colors with two different brands of dye. The slight difference in these matched colors gives the piece an amazing depth.

Lori's Lavender Fields

Lori followed the Sweater Map for Jacob's Windows (page 68) to produce this colorful up-and-down cardigan. She used more elaborate color changes and stitch patterns, altered the collar with a triangle edging, added stockinette stitch facings to the hem and cuffs, and narrowed the sleeves a bit.

Inspired by a visit to a local lavender farm, Lori dyed superfine merino fiber the same rich colors, then spun it into a variety of 2-ply DK-weight yarns. She chose colors for the Fair Isle pattern by randomly pulling balls of yarn from a basket of her handspun. She charted out some of the more complicated stitch patterns (such as the leaves in the center of the bodice) on graph paper, but for the most part, she worked spontaneously, enjoying the colorful yarns playing off one another as the sweater grew.

Beach Sweater

This roomy pullover is loosely related to Angel Wing Lace Float (page 104) in that the bodice is a combination of up-and-down and side-to-side construction. The Beach Sweater's bodice is wider, its bodice front and back are worked in three panels that are sewn together (similar to Laurie's Panel Jacket on page 112), the side-to-side panels are narrower, and the sleeves are tapered like Mary's Classic Crew (page 15). The square-bottomed V neckline sports an overlapping stockinette stitch edging, and the hem and cuff are edged with classic ribbing. I purposefully knitted a naïve-styled rolled edge at the neckline to reflect the fact that this was my very first sweater from my own handspun yarn.

The color blocks on the center back and front represent my transition from knitting with other spinners' and dyers' yarns to spinning and dyeing the yarn myself. The first square at the bottom of the back is Sandy's yarn. I spun subsequent squares from Sandy's and Lynn's fibers in colors reminiscent of the willows, waves, and sky I saw on my morning walks with my dogs in Cannon Beach, Oregon. At last, the center front yarn directly below the neckline is all my own yarn dyed in the greens of the dune grass. The blue yarn of the rest of the bodice is a carded blend of white Corriedale wool and some wild blue and purple mohairs and silks from Sandy's stash.

Autumn Vest

I combined both crochet and knitting in this side-to-side variation (below) of the Rectangle Vest (page 75). I crocheted the back in a shell pattern, then I knitted the fronts from the side seams to the center, matching the gauge of the crochet. I added slits for crochet inserts at the hemline and worked a V-neck shaping along the way. Because knitted stitches stretch more than crochet stitches, the front looks longer and appears to curve at the hem. This adds an unexpected design detail.

The yarn is handdyed superwash colonial wool fiber in a variety of shades that remind me of the golden tones of autumn equinox sunlight on the fading green of the forest canopy. I spun the yarn into active twist singles and alternated bands of stockinette stitch and reverse stockinette stitch so that the knitting would torque into a lively zigzag pattern.

Debbie's Tunic

Debbie's tunic (above) is a sleeveless version of the Bouclé Boat Neck (page 48). She embellished the simple bodice at the armholes and hem with two different sizes of triangle edging (also used in Friendship Sweater on page 123), and finished the neckline with single crochet.

Debbie handspun a laceweight singles yarn from her carded blends of handdyed wool and silk, varying the colors throughout. She used large needles (size 10) to knit small lots of yarn right off the bobbin of her spinning wheel within several days of spinning. The active twist in this fresh yarn causes the stitches to torque, making them collapse into each other for a springy textured garter stitch fabric.

Mary Kaiser's Daisy Stitch Vest

Mary's Daisy Stitch Vest is a variation of Alina's Basketweave Coat (page 53). Mary's vest is shorter and has a V neckline, but it is worked up and down and has the same armhole shaping and straight lines.

Mary used her active-twist handspun yarn to knit the vest in two colorways. To balance the torque in the active yarn, Mary used the Daisy Stitch pattern from Barbara Walker's *Treasury*. She offset the daisy motifs on the front of the vests to produce a supple fabric. For the back, she aligned the motifs to produce a textured rib pattern. She finished with a crocheted shell edging.

Chinese Tree of Life

This colorful cardigan is similar in construction to the Angel Wing Lace Float (page 104). I started by knitting a sample swatch of a mosaic pattern. That swatch grew into the right front panel. I then knitted a panel for the other front and three panels for the back. I joined the back panels with mattress-stitch seams, then joined the fronts to the back at the shoulder. For the side panels, I picked up stitches along the selvedges, working from the wrong side of the piece so that the colorful chain selvedge would show on the right side. I continued the side panels into the sleeves, and added the hem edging and collar at the end.

The center panels of the bodice and bottom band are knitted in worsted-weight handspun yarns. The sleeves and collar are commercial brushed mohair that I dyed to complement the other colors. The yarns in the background of the central design are La Lana Wools' naturally dyed Forever Random Blends. The foreground yarns are spun by Sandy Sitzman and dyed by yours truly. The motif of three lines that appears in the center edging by the collar and the bottom band is the trigram for Heaven (without) from the Chinese I-Ching. The spiral motif symbolizes Earth (within) and appears in petroglyphs worldwide.

Crystal's Wild Thing

Crystal varied the Up-and-Down Classic Crew (page 15) by cropping the length, widening the bodice, and shaping a ballet neckline. Then she added a wildly ruffled collar by picking up stitches around the neckline stitch for stitch. She then doubled the number of stitches on the first round, and again when the collar was half the finished length. Crystal worked the collar in reverse stockinette stitch so that the stockinette-stitch side would show when the collar folded over. She worked her ruffled sleeve cuffs in stockinette stitch throughout, doubling the number of stitches only once. As a final touch, Crystal used waxed silk thread to sew African trade beads along the hemline.

Crystal's fabric is based on Butterscotch Tweed Worsted by Weaving Southwest alternated with Whisper by Crystal Palace, India by Lana Grossa, and Brazilian PomPom by Schachenmayer Nomotta.

Abbreviations

beg	begin(s); beginning
BO	bind off
CC	contrast color
cm	centimeter(s)
cn	cable needle
CO	cast on
cont	continue(s); continuing
dec(s)	decrease(s); decreasing
dpn	double-pointed needles
foll	follow(s); following
g	gram(s)
inc(s)	increase(s); increasing
k	knit
k1f&b	knit into the front and back of same st
kwise	knitwise, as if to knit
m	marker(s)
MC	main color
mm	millimeter(s)
M1	make one (increase)
p	purl
p1f&b	purl into front and back of same st
patt(s)	pattern(s)
psso	pass slipped st over
pwise	purlwise, as if to purl
rem	remain(s); remaining

rep	repeat(s); repeating
rev St st	reverse stockinette stitch
rnd(s)	round(s)
RS	right side
sl	slip
sl st	slip st (slip 1 st pwise unless otherwise indicated)
ssk	slip 2 sts kwise, one at a time, from the left needle to right needle, insert left needle tip through both front loops and knit together from this position (1 st decrease)
St st	stockinette stitch
tbl	through back loop
tog	together
WS	wrong side
wyb	with yarn in back
wyf	with yarn in front
yd	yard(s)
yo	yarnover
*	repeat starting point
* *	repeat all instructions between asterisks
( )	alternate measurements and/or instructions
[ ]	work instructions as a group a specified number of times

Bind-Offs

Cable Bind-Off

This bind-off looks lovely with seed stitch or other alternating k1, p1 patterns. Ellen discovered it while trying to make a textured and decorative edge for her seed stitch knitting. It makes an irregular edge and is flexible. It pairs with the knit/purl cable cast-on (page 132).

Seed Stitch Version

If the first stitch is a purl stitch (Figure 1), knit 1. *Bring the yarn forward between the stitches (Figure 2), return the first stitch to the left needle and p2tog (Figure 3), bring the yarn to the back and return new stitch to the left needle (Figure 4), and k2tog. Repeat from *.

   If the first stitch is a knit stitch, purl it and continue from k2tog (Figure 5).

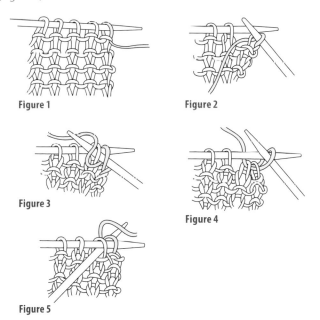

Figure 1   **Figure 2**

Figure 3   **Figure 4**

Figure 5

K1, P1 Rib Version

If you want to prevent this bind-off from splaying, work it with a needle one or two sizes smaller than the one used to knit the rib. I used the splay as a design featre on the collar of my version of Zylie's Cardigan (page 89).

   If the first stitch is a purl stitch, purl 1. *Bring the yarn to the back, slip the stitch just made onto the left needle, k2tog, bring yarn to front, slip the stitch just made onto the left needle, p2tog. Repeat from *.

   If the first stitch is a knit stitch, knit it and continue from k2tog.

Chain Bind-Off

This is the basic bind-off that almost everyone uses. It has very little stretch so it makes a good stabilizing seam for shoulders. It can also be used as a decorative edge for visible seams. Pair this bind-off with the chain cast-on (page 133).

Knitting Needle Method

Knit the first two stitches. Lift the first stitch over the second stitch (Figure 1) and off the needle (Figure 2), *k1, pass the previous st over; repeat from * across the row. Pull yarn through the last loop to anchor.

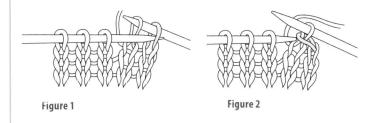

Figure 1   **Figure 2**

Crochet Hook Method

This method is quicker. Using a crochet hook similar in size to the needles you knit with, insert the hook into the first stitch on the needle, bring the working yarn over the crochet hook, and pull a loop though—1 stitch on hook. *Insert the hook into next stitch, bring working yarn over the crochet hook, and pull a loop through both stitches (that stitch and thte stitch on the hook). that stitch and the stitch on the hook. Repeat from *, pulling each loop open on the hook before gently pulling through the next loop to prevent the loops from being too tight. Cut yarn and pull tail through the last loop to anchor.

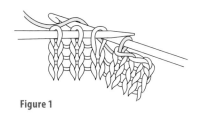

Figure 1

Loop Bind-Off

This sewn bind-off mimics a backward-loop cast-on and produces an elastic edge. It's wonderful for shoulder seams because it is not as bulky as a chain bind-off. Pair this bind-off with the backward-loop cast-on (page 133).

Measure your working yarn tail and cut it a little more than four times the width of the knitting to be bound off. Thread the tail into a tapestry needle. Working from right to left, insert threaded needle knitwise into first stitch (Figure 1). Pull yarn through and slip this stitch off the knitting needle. Insert threaded needle from left to right (knitwise) through the next stitch, then left to right (purlwise) into the first stitch (Figure 2), then slip that stitch off the knitting needle. Keeping the working yarn above the stitches as shown, *insert threaded needle into the first loop of the next stitch on the left needle from left to right, then into the second loop of the previous stitch from left to right (Figure 3), and slip that stitch off the needle. Repeat from * until the last stitch is worked. Anchor yarn at the end of the row by running it through the last stitch one more time.

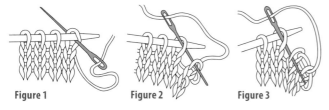

Figure 1　　　**Figure 2**　　　**Figure 3**

𝒯𝒾𝓅 **Minimizing Stair Steps When Binding Off**

I personally don't care for the stair-stepped effect left from binding off more than one stitch every two rows. To get a smooth edge, I work as follows. *On the return row after working the first set of bind-offs, don't work the last stitch—there will be 1 stitch on the right needle. Turn the work and slip the first stitch to the right needle—there will be 2 stitches on the right needle (Figure 1). Pass the unworked stitch over the slipped stitch and off the needle (Figure 2). Bind off the specified number of stitches in the second set. Repeat from * for each set of bind-off stitches.

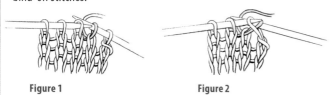

Figure 1　　　　　**Figure 2**

Cast-Ons

Cable Cast-On

This is a very nice looking cast-on, one that's easy to pick up stitches into or sew into a seam—it leaves very little bulk. It works well in conjunction with nonstretching stitch patterns such as linen stitch. Knitting from the top down, I like to use this cast-on at the shoulder seam line or to make up the stitches at the bottom of the neckline opening of a wide neckline. Pair this cast-on with the cable bind-off (page 131).

Tie a slipknot and cinch the loop down on a needle held in your left hand. Insert the tip of the right needle into the slipknot, wind yarn around the needle knitwise, pull a loop though, and place it in front of the slipknot on the left needle—there will be 2 stitches on the needle. *Insert the right needle between the two stitches on the left needle (Figure 1), gently pull the working yarn to gauge, wind the yarn around the needle knitwise, pull up a new loop (Figure 2), and place this loop on the left needle (Figure 3)—3 stitches on the needle. Repeat from * for desired number of stitches, always working between the first two stitches on the left needle.

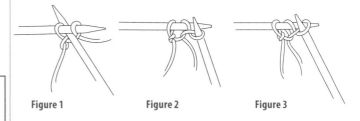

Figure 1　　　**Figure 2**　　　**Figure 3**

𝒯𝒾𝓅 **Flexible Cable Cast-On**

The cable cast-on is often thought to be inflexible and not suitable for areas that need stretch. However, the trick to making a more flexible cable cast-on is inserting the shaft of the needle (not just the point) between the first two stitches on the left needle before you adjust the yarn to gauge; that way, you're not forcing the needle through a too-small space when making the next stitch.

Knit/Purl Cable Cast-On

This version of the cable cast-on alternates the direction from which you enter between the loops. Pair this cast-on with the cable bind-off (page 131).

Work this variation as for the cable cast-on, but for every other stitch, insert the right needle from back to front between the first two stitches on the left needle as shown, and wrap the yarn around the needle purlwise.

Chain Cast-On

This cast-on is worked with a crochet hook. Pair it with the chain bind-off (page 131).

Make a slipknot on the crochet hook and hold it in your right hand. Hold a knitting needle and yarn in your left hand. *Bring the yarn under the needle and use the crochet hook to grab a loop over the top of the needle, and pull it through the slipknot (Figure 1). Bring the yarn back under the needle in preparation for the next stitch. Repeat from * for the required number of stitches minus one. Transfer the loop on the crochet hook to the needle for the last stitch.

Figure 1

Backward-Loop Cast-On

This simple cast-on, also called the "simple" or "e" cast-on, makes a minimal and flexible edge that's ideal for fishbone- and mattress-stitch seams. Because it has a tendency to splay, it is perfect when you want the cast-on row to have some widthwise stretch, as in many lace patterns. Pair it with the loop bind-off (page 132).

Tie a slipknot and cinch the loop down on a needle held in your right hand. *Wrap the working yarn around your left thumb clockwise so that the yarn coming from the needle is on top of the circle of

Figure 1

yarn around the thumb. Insert the right needle under the in front of your thumb (Figure 1) and slip the loop off your thumb and tighten it onto the needle. Repeat from * for the desired number of stitches. This forms the stitches knitwise on the needle. If you want to form the stitches purlwise on the needle, wrap the yarn around your thumb counterclockwise (Figure 2). Note: If the first stitch of the row comes undone when you try to knit it, wrap your yarn in the opposite direction. You only need to do this on the first stitch.

Figure 2

Long-Tail Cast-On

This flexible cast-on is a favorite of many. It is flexible enough to use for cuffs, but to ensure that the edge isn't too tight, stretch the stitches out on the needle as you go. The yarn should maintain its loft so that the yarn in the cast-on edge looks as fluffy as the yarn in the skein.

Wind off a length of working yarn that is four times longer than your desired row. Tie a slipknot and cinch the loop down on the needle, letting the long tail hang down. Pinch your index finger and thumb together and insert them between the working yarn and the tail, so that the tail hangs over your thumb and the working yarn hangs over your index finger. Hold both yarns with your remaining fingers to tension them and hold your palm upwards, making a V of yarn (Figure 1). *Bring the needle up through the loop on your thumb (Figure 2), grab a loop from the first strand around your index finger, and bring the needle back down through the loop on your thumb (Figure 3). Drop the loop off your thumb and return your thumb to the V configuration (Figure 4), tightening the resulting stitch on the needle as you do so. Repeat from * for the desired number of stitches.

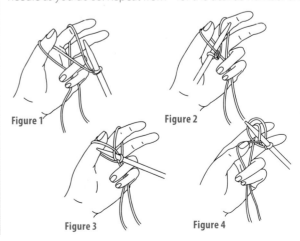

Figure 1

Figure 2

Figure 3

Figure 4

Provisional Cast-Ons

The ability to create a provisional row is an indispensable design tool. It enables you to begin knitting fabric at any point in the pattern, then pick up stitches and knit in the opposite direction with very little fuss.

Provisional Chain Cast-On

This is the simplest provisional cast-on. Work it exactly as the chain cast-on on page 133, but use waste yarn for the cast-on stitches. When you have the desired number of stitches, pull a long waste yarn tail through the last stitch on your needle to temporarily hold it. Work as usual with the main yarn. When you are ready to remove the provisional cast-on, extract the tail from the last cast-on stitch and slowly remove the waste yarn, placing the live stitches on a needle as they are exposed. Note that there will be one less exposed stitch than was cast on. Simply increase one stitch in the first row to return to the original stitch count.

Invisible Provisional Cast-On

Also called "the professional's cast-on," this cast-on takes longer to learn than the provisional chain method, but is well worth the time and effort. It is incredibly fast in practiced hands and leaves a flaw-lessly invisible provisional row. Note: This cast-on also stands alone as an elastic edge for k1, p1 rib. Just substitute a length of your main yarn for the waste yarn.

Tie a slipknot near the end of your working yarn and cinch it down on your needle. Cut a piece of waste yarn as long as the row you wish to cast on plus 12 inches, and tie a slipknot near one end of it. Snug this slipknot next to the first one. Hold the tails of both yarns in your right hand to keep them out of the way. Coming from behind, insert your left index finger and thumb between the working yarn and the waste yarn, twist the yarns 90° counterclockwise and wrap the working yarn over the needle (Figure 1). *Twist the yarns 180° clockwise and wrap the working yarn over the needle (Figure 2). Twist the yarns 180° counterclockwise and wrap the working yarn over the needle (Figure 3). Repeat from * until you have the desired number

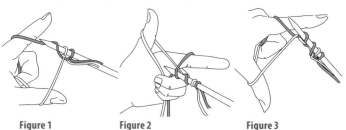

Figure 1   **Figure 2**   **Figure 3**

of stitches, being careful never to wrap the waste yarn around the needle. Work the last stitch as a backward-loop cast-on (page 133) to anchor the provisional stitches in place.

Make sure the waste yarn is caught under the first stitch to anchor the loop when you begin knitting. Every other stitch will be twisted on the needle; to straighten them, simply knit them through their back loops. When you're ready to work the cast-on stitches in the opposite direction, insert a needle through the loops held by the waste yarn and remove the waste yarn.

Crochet

Single Crochet

Working from right to left, insert hook into a stitch and draw up a loop on the hook. Bring the yarn over the hook and draw this loop through the one already on the hook—there will be 1 loop on the hook. *Insert the hook into the next stitch to the left, draw up a loop (Figure 1), bring the yarn over the hook again and draw this loop through the two loops on the hook (Figure 2). Repeat from * for each stitch.

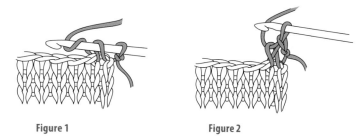

Figure 1   **Figure 2**

Crochet Chain

Make a slipknot and place it on the hook. Yarn over the hook and draw it through the loop of the slipknot. *Yarn over the hook and draw it through the last loop formed. Repeat from * for each stitch.

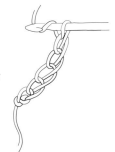

Decreases

Single Left Decrease

In a left-slanting decrease, the first stitch entered will lie on top of the second.

Slip two stitches knitwise, one at a time, from the left needle to the right needle (Figure 1), insert the tip of the left needle into the front loops of both stitches and knit them together through their back loops with the right needle (Figure 2).

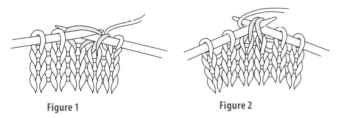

Figure 1   **Figure 2**

Single Right Decrease

In a right-slanting decrease, the second stitch on the needle will of lie on top of the first.

Knit two stitches together by entering the second stitch first, then the first stitch In one motion.

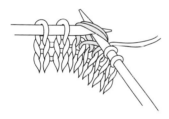

Paired Decreases

Paired decreases are made by working two types of single decreases in the same row, a single left decrease and a single right decrease. The two decreases will angle toward each other. Knitting from right to left, work the single left decrease first, then the single right decrease. These decreases can be side by side as they would appear on a sleeve knitted in the round, or they can be at opposite ends of a row, such as a sleeve knitted flat.

Increases

Lifted Increase

This increase is virtually invisible, especially when used with stockinette.

Insert the right needle into the back loop of the stitch below the next stitch that presents itself. Knit this stitch (Figure 1), then knit the stitch on the needle and slip it off the left needle (Figure 2).

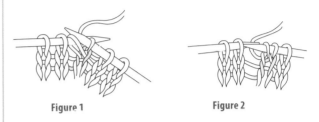

Figure 1   **Figure 2**

Backward-Loop Cast-On Increase

This is a good increase to use with garter stitch.

Simply make a backward-loop cast-on (page 133) to create a stitch.

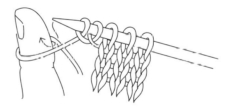

Pick Up and Knit

Picking up stitches into an existing selvedge is one way to minimize the number of seams you'll need to sew at the end of a project. As long as you maintain your stitch gauge as you pick up stitches, the pieces will fit together without gaps or puckers.

When picking up stitches along a garter stitch fabric, where there are twice the number of rows per inch as there are stitches per inch, pick up one stitch for every two rows of knitting. This is where a chain stitch selvedge (page 139) comes in handy—you'll pick up one stitch for every chain along the selvedge. When picking up stitches along a stockinette stitch fabric, where there are more rows than stitches per inch, you'll want to pick up about three stitches for every four

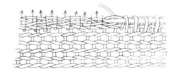

Figure 1

rows of knitting (Figure 1). If you have a chain stitch selvedge, pick up two stitches into every third chain. If you have a stockinette stitch selvedge, you may need to skip some of the selvedge stitches as you pick up. Skip stitches at regular intervals for a smooth pick-up edge. If you're unsure about the number of stitches to pick up, measure the length of the pick-up edge and calculate what your cast-on number would be for length. Or place a vertical pin every inch along the edge, then pick up your gauge per inch between the pins.

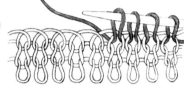

To pick up stitches along a backward-loop cast-on edge, pick up one stitch in each cast-on loop (Figure 2). The pick-up row is nearly invisible on the front of the work.

Figure 2

Seams

Crochet Chain Stitch Seam

Also called the "crochet slip stitch seam," this technique makes a very sturdy seam. It's a good choice for fragile yarn because only small amounts of yarn are pulled through the fabric at a time. I like to use the crochet chain stitch seam to decoratively join chain selvedges on the outside of sweaters. The technique is the same whether you're working along selvedge edges (as for the side seams of sweaters worked up and down) or bind-off edges (as for the shoulder seams of sweaters worked up and down).

Before you begin, lightly steam the edges to make them easier to handle. Hold the pieces to be seamed parallel to each other with their right sides together if you want the seam on the inside of the garment; hold the pieces with their wrong sides together if you want a decorative seam on the outside of the garment. Be careful not to work too tightly as this will cause the seam to pucker.

Insert the crochet hook under the first chain on each piece, draw a loop of yarn through the fabric and onto the hook, *insert the hook into the next pair of chain stitches to the left as illustrated, and draw a loop of yarn through the fabric and the loop on the hook. Repeat from * for each stitch, pulling the loops to match the tension of the fabric. At the end, cut the yarn and pull the tail through the last loop on the hook.

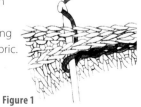

Figure 1

Fishbone Stitch

The fishbone stitch is very fluid and moves with the fabric. It is nearly invisible when sewn with the working yarn. For a decorative laced-up look, use a contrasting color yarn. For an invisible flat seam, use it with a garter stitch or seed stitch selvedge.

Lay the pieces to be seamed side by side on a flat surface with their right sides facing up. Anchor the tail of the seaming yarn to one piece. Make a simple whipstitch (page 139) at the base of the two fabric pieces—this will serve as the first horizontal stitch.

If you're working along selvedge edges, begin on the right side of the seam and insert the needle under one-half selvedge stitch from back to front, then insert the needle under one-half selvedge stitch directly opposite on the left side of the seam (Figure 1). Gently pull the working yarn to pull the two sides together. Repeat from * for each stitch.

If you're working along two bind-off edges, *insert the tapestry needle between the bound-off loops of one stitch on the far side (Figure 2), pull yarn through. Bring the yarn over the bound-off edges to the near side and insert needle under both loops of the adjacent bound-off stitch on the near side. Gently pull working yarn to pull the two sides together. Repeat from * for each stitch. You can also make the seam by working under both loops on both sides or under single loops on both sides.

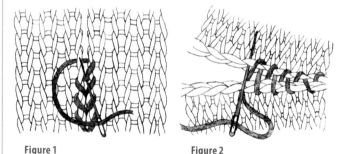

Figure 1　　　　　　　**Figure 2**

Kitchener Stitch

The Kitchener stitch provides a seamless join for live stitches by mimicking a row of knitting. You'll need to have the same number of stitches in the two pieces to be joined, and each set of stitches needs to be on a separate needle. Thread a tapestry needle with yarn four times the length of the row to be worked. I prefer to use the tail of the yarn I've been working with so that I don't have to work in extra ends, but this isn't always possible.

Hold the needles parallel to each other with the right sides of the knitting facing up. For stockinette stitch, work from right to left as follows:

Step 1: Bring the tapestry needle through the first stitch on the front needle from back to front and leave that stitch on the needle (Figure 1).

Step 2. Bring the tapestry needle through the first stitch on the back needle from back to front and leave that stitch on the needle (Figure 2).

Step 3. Bring the tapestry needle through the first front stitch from back to front and slip that stitch off the needle, then bring tapestry needle through the next front stitch from back to front and leave that stitch on the needle (Figure 3).

Step 4. Bring the tapestry needle through the first back stitch from front to back and slip that stitch off the needle, then bring the tapestry needle through the next back stitch from back to front and leave that stitch on the needle (Figure 4).

Repeat Steps 3 and 4 until no stitches remain on the needles,

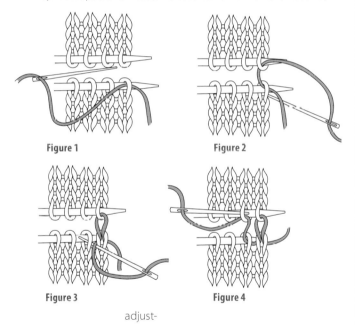

Figure 1

Figure 2

Figure 3

Figure 4

adjusting the tension to match the rest of the knitting as you go.

To graft garter stitch, work as follows:

Align the two pieces to be joined as follows: The back fabric should have the last garter ridge on the wrong side of the fabric. The front fabric should have the last garter ridge on the front side of the fabric.

Step 1: Bring the tapestry needle through the first stitch on the front needle from back to front and leave that stitch on the needle (Figure 1).

Step 2: Bring the tapestry needle through the first stitch on the back

needle from front to back and leave that stitch on the needle (Figure 2).

Step 3: Bring the tapestry needle through the first front stitch from front to back and slip that stitch off the needle, then bring the tapestry needle through the next front stitch from back to front (Figure 3).

Step 4: Bring the tapestry needle through the first back stitch from back to front and slip that stitch off the needle, then bring the tapestry needle through the next back stitch from front to back and leave that stitch on the needle (Figure 4).

Repeat Steps 3 and 4 until no stitches remain on the needles.

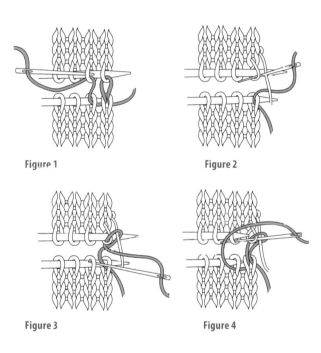

Figure 1

Figure 2

Figure 3

Figure 4

Tip ___Kitchener Stitch___

I prefer to work the Kitchener stitch on flat fabric pieces by removing the stitches from the needles and placing them on firm, smooth waste yarn, such as cotton warp yarn or nylon string, that won't be easily caught up in the sewing process.

Mattress Stitch

The mattress stitch is the most commonly used stitch for joining all types of edges when there is the same number of stitches on each edge. It turns the selvedge stitches to the wrong side of the garment and makes a flexible join that moves with the fabric. Use this stitch to join stockinette, chain, or garter stitch selvedges. And use it to join cast-on and bind-off edges.

Lay the pieces to be joined side by side on a flat surface with the right sides facing upward and the lower edges (such as the hemline or cuff) at the bottom. Because I'm right handed, I like to orient my work so that the bottom edges are to the right, and I work from right to left. Thread a tapestry needle with yarn and, working from bottom to top, catch the horizontal bars between a ladder of stitches on one piece, then catch the corresponding horizontal bars on the other. Pull the seaming yarn in the direction of the seam and snug it just tight enough to cause the edge stitches to turn under and the two pieces of fabric to snug together. Stockinette and chain selvedges have a tendency to roll under. Put your free hand under the seam and unroll the fabric as you work to ensure you see the stitches clearly and follow a single ladder line.

When joining chain selvedges, catch the double horizontal bar that separates each chain loop from the rest of the fabric. This will cause the entire selvedge stitch on each piece to turn under into the seam allowance

When joining stockinette stitch selvedges, you can choose to have the entire selvedge stitch or just half of it turn under into the seam allowance. For a full stitch seam allowance, catch the double horizontal bar that separates the selvedge stitch from the rest of the fabric just as for a chain selvedge. For a half-stitch seam allowance work into the centers of the selvedge stitches.

When joining pieces with garter stitch selvedges, the two pieces will fit together in a flat seam. Notice that for every two rows

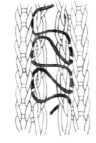

Mattress stitch on chain selvedges

Mattress stitch on stockinette stitch with full stitch seam allowance

Mattress stitch on stockinette stitch with one-half stitch seam allowance

of knitting there is a loop that extends out the side of the selvedge. Catch this loop, then catch the corresponding loop on the other side of the seam. Pull the yarn just tight enough to bring the fabric together so that the loops sit one on top of another, like the teeth of a zipper.

When joining bind-off edges, *bring the tapestry needle beneath a pair of chains on one edge, pull the yarn through, insert the needle beneath the pair of chains on the other piece. Repeat from * to the end of the seam. You can use a firm hand when pulling the seaming yarn in this case; it's difficult to pull the yarn too tightly.

When used to join cast-on edges, the mattress stitch is sewn much like the Kitchener stitch. It will make an invisible join on a backward-loop cast-on edge that has the stability of a sewn seam. The final appearance of the seam is determined by the tension of the yarn as you pull it through. You can pull it as though you were grafting with Kitchener stitch, making the seam row in the same gauge as the rest of the knitting, or you can pull the yarn tight so that the seam row largely disappears.

*Enter the first stitch of the cast-on row of the top piece from back to front, then enter the first stitch of the cast-on row of the bottom piece from front to back, and at the same time enter the next stitch on the lower piece from back to front (working a scooping motion with the tapestry needle). Return to the first stitch in the upper piece and enter the same stitch from front to back, at the same time enter the next stitch on the upper piece from back to front (using the same scooping motion). Repeat from * to the end of the seam.

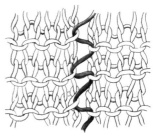

Mattress stitch on garter stitch

Mattress stitch on bind-off edges

Mattress stitch on cast-on edges

Three-Needle Bind-Off

Although this is called a bind-off, it's used to bind off two pieces of fabric together simultaneously, forming a seam. The seam is very firm, much like a crochet seam, but less bulky. You'll need to have the stitches for each piece on a separate needle—if your stitches are on holders, transfer them to needles. I like to use either circular or double-pointed needles for this because I don't have to worry which way the points are facing when I return the live stitches to the needles.

The two pieces of fabric to be joined should each have the same number of live stitches on needles. To place the seam on the inside of the garment, hold the pieces with their right sides facing each other. To place the seam on the outside of the fabric as a decorative seam, hold the pieces with their wrong sides facing each other. In either case, hold the needles in your left hand with the points facing to the right.

Insert a third needle through the first stitch on each needle, wrap the yarn around the needle, draw a loop through both stitches, and slip them both off the needle—there will be one stitch on the right needle. *Insert this needle into the first stitch on each needle, warp the yarn around the needle, draw a loop through, and slip these stitches off the needle—there will now be two stitches on the right needle. Lift the first stitch up and over the second (as in a chain bind-off; page 131), and off the needle. Repeat from * for the desired number of stitches.

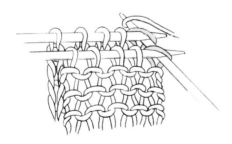

Whipstitch

Place two edges side by side so that you have two parallel lines of chains with the chains lining up in pairs. With a tapestry needle threaded with a length of yarn, enter the chain on the right side from front to back, then enter the chain to the left from back to front. Pull yarn though. Repeat with the next pair of chains to the end. Keep a tension that is firm enough to pull

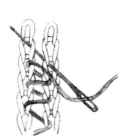

the two pieces of fabric together but still allows the chains to lie flat beside one another. This same method can be worked with bound-off edges.

Selvedge Stitches

There are a number of different ways to work selvedge stitches, and the way you choose can greatly facilitate working seams (or picking up stitches) later. Different types of selvedge stitches work best with different types of seaming stitches. Therefore, you'll want to decide on the type of selvedge stitches and seams in the early stages of your design process.

Chain Stitch Selvedge

This selvedge is made by slipping the first stitch of every row (knitwise on knit rows; purlwise on purl rows). It forms a chain-like loop for every two rows of knitting that is easy to see, and easy to sew or pick up stitches into. I like to pair a chain stitch selvedge with a mattress stitch seam (page 138) when I want the selvedge stitches to turn toward the wrong side of a garment; I pair it with a crochet chain stitch seam (page 136) when I want the selvedges stitches to be visible on the right side of the garment.

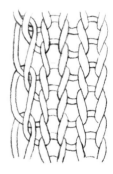

Stockinette Stitch Selvedge

This selvedge is made by knitting the first and last stitch of every right-side row and purling them on wrong-side rows. If you're working stockinette stitch, you won't be able to distinguish the selvedge stitches from the body of the piece.

This type of selvedge produces very little bulk and produces an elastic edge that is particularly well suited to bias panels or curved edges. Mattress and fishbone stitches (pages 138 and 136, respectively) are good choices for seaming stockinette selvedges.

Garter Stitch Selvedge

The garter stitch selvedge is made by knitting the first and last stitch of every row (right side and wrong side). I like to pair garter stitch selvedges with the mattress-stitch seam for garter stitch (page 138) to produce a flat seam that is completely reversible.

Short-Rows

Short-rows can be used to shape fabric from within so that the cast-on and bind-off edges remain straight. Linda used short-rows to shape the sleeve taper on her One-Piece Turtleneck (page 60). Short-rows also can be used to shape V necks in side-to-side knitting or shoulder seams on up-and-down garments to avoid the stair-stepping edge left by groups of bind-offs and cast-ons. A short-row is formed by knitting up to a particular stitch, wrapping that stitch to prevent a hole from forming, then turning and knitting back from that spot.

To work a short-row, work to the turn point, slip the next stitch purlwise to the right needle and bring the yarn to the front (Figure 1). Slip the same stitch back to the left needle (Figure 2). Turn the work around and bring the yarn into position for the next stitch, wrapping the yarn around the slipped stitch as you do so.

Hide the wraps when you come to them on subsequent rows as follows: On a knit stitch, insert the right needle under the wrap from the bottom up and then into the wrapped stitch as usual. Knit the two together, making sure the new stitch comes out under the wrap. On a purl stitch, insert the right needle from under the back of the wrap to lift the wrap onto the left needle, then purl the wrap together with the wrapped stitch.

Figure 1

Figure 2

Ripping Out: As We Create, So Do We Destroy

Mistakes are inevitable, even on the simplest of fabrics. Sometimes, small mistakes can be overlooked and will not affect the overall success of a garment. But most of the time success depends on perfection and perfection often involves fixing mistakes.

Small Mistakes

If the mistake involves just a few stitches, you can usually fix it without ripping out much knitting.

The mistake is in the same row you're working on

Leave the work on the needles, unknit to the mistake, rectify the problem, and continue knitting from there. I've been known to unknit several rows because I find it safer than taking the work off the needles and ripping out.

The mistake is a row or two below

Knit to the stitch (or stitches) immediately above the mistake, drop the stitch (or stitches) down to the mistake, use a crochet hook to pick up the stitches correctly, and continue knitting as usual. This method is especially effective for changing knits to purls and vice versa and for picking up dropped stitches.

Big Mistakes

If the mistake involves a large number of stitches or stitches that involve increases and/or decreases, it is usually easiest to take the stitches off the needles and rip out the knitting (and I'd be lying if I said I hadn't ripped out several hundred miles of rows in my knitting career).

Anchor the Fabric and Rip

Find a circular needle in the same—or preferably smaller—size than the one you've been knitting with. Locate the row you need to rip to and work the circular needle into every stitch of the row below the row that has the mistake to anchor the stitches. This needle will anchor the stitches so that you can't inadvertently rip out too many rows. Rip down to this needle, then continue knitting (without duplicating the mistake) as usual.

If you don't have a smaller circular needle, you can thread smooth waste yarn on a tapestry needle and run it through the stitches below the row with the mistake. Rip out to the row of stitches on the waste yarn, return the stitches to your needles, and continue on your way.

Anchoring the fabric is especially helpful with those frustrating yarns that tend to snag and then let go suddenly (like brushed mohair), causing more stitches to be raveled than intended.

Ripping out can be fun.

Anchor the Fabric and Cut

Sometimes you'll find that you've made a mistake way down in the first few rows of knitting, especially if you're working an unfamiliar stitch pattern. Instead of ripping out all the way down, you can cut off the part that isn't quite right and continue knitting on the part of the fabric that looks good. This can be done most easily with stockinette-, seed- or garter-stitch fabric but can also be done with some repeat patterns.

With a plain fabric such as stockinette stitch, anchor the yarn above the mistake. Then carefully cut across a row or two below the anchor and remove the knitting with the mistake. Finish it by picking up stitch for stitch and knitting in the opposite direction, or start the piece over again and join it to the good piece of knitting with Kitchener stitch. I prefer the second option for rectifying intricate patterns where a change of knitting direction would be obvious, such as Fair Isle, stranded color patters, or cables. I would much rather Kitchener stitch one row than rip out fifty and reknit them.

No Anchor, Just Rip

Of course sometimes the mistake is so great that a total tear down must occur, such as casting on too many or too few stitches. When that happens, I just try to get it over with as soon as possible!

Resources

Artisan Yarns Here are a few sources for artisan yarns. Find more at a Wool Festival near you at http://www.woolfestival.com/bydate2.php.

Botanical Shades
Yarns dyed with natural dyes (Tregellys Fibers and Shades, formerly). Jodie McKenzie, PO Box 175, Shelburne Falls, MA 01370
413-625-9492
botanicalshades@earthlink.net
www.eweandme.com/yarn.html

Buckwheat Bridge Angoras
Registered Angora Goats and lovely mohair yarn
Sara Healy and Dan Melamed
518-537-4487
slhdem@valstar.net
bwbagoats.com

Capistrano Fiber Arts
Lori Lawson
paintspinknit.blogspot.com
CapFibArt@aol.com

Chasing Rainbows
Nancy Finn, 1700 Hilltop Dr., Willits, CA 95490
707-459-8558
yarns/chas-rainbows.html
crownmountainfarms.com/html/yarns/chas-rainbow.html

Kid Hollow Farm
Beautiful handdyed yarns
Pat and Steve Harder, PO Box 101, Free Union, VA 22940
434-973-8070
kidhollow@cstone.net

La Lana Wools
136-C Paseo Norte, Taos, NM 87571
505-758-9631
lalanawools.com

Lisa Milliman, Dicentra Designs
dicentra@earthlink.net
home.earthlink.net/~dicentra/index
crownmountainfarms.com/html/artists/lisaMilliman

Lynne Vogel LTD
Limited-edition handdyed fibers and handspun yarns
handspuncentral.blogspot.com

Morehouse Farm
Margrit Lohrer, In Sheep's Clothing (shop), 2 Rock City Road, Milan, NY 12571
customer service 845-758-3710
morehousefarm.com/KnittingEssentials/Yarn

NW Wools
Linda Berning, 3524 SW Troy St. (located in Multnomah Village), Portland, OR 97219
503-244-5024
nwwools@ccwebster.net

Peace of Yarn
Luxury yarn and fiber from around the world
info@peaceofyarn.com
peaceofyarn.com

Persimmon Tree
Greta Dise, 12901 Pleasant Valley Road, Glen Rock, PA 17327
717-235-5140
Persimmon2@juno.com
angoragoat.com/persimmon/fiber

Spinning a Dream
Becky Smith
860-283-0362
spinning-a-dream.com

Three Waters Farm
Handmade and handdyed yarns and fiber
PO Box 100, Saxapahaw, NC 27340
336-376-0378
threewatersfarm.com/Zcart

Tintagel Farm
Leslie and Ron Orndorff, RR2, Box 2262, Glenville, PA 17329
717-235-2814
tintagel@aol.com

Woolgatherings
Sandy Sitzman
http://www.twistedmom.blogspot.com/

Suggested Reading (a short list of valuable books)
Budd, Ann. *The Knitter's Handy Book of Sweater Patterns*. Loveland, Colorado: Interweave Press, 2002. Standard sizing.
Dowde, Jenny. *Freeform Knitting and Crochet*. Binda NSW Australia: Sally Milner Publishing, 2004. Knitting outside the box.
Epstein, Nicky. *Knitting on the Edge*. New York: Sixth and Spring, 2004. Embellishments.
---. *Knitting Over the Edge* New York: Sixth and Spring, 2005. More embellishments.
Eskesen, Elaine. *Dyeing to Knit*. Rockport, Maine: Down East Books, 2005. Dyeing artisan yarns.
Hiatt, June Hemmons. *The Principles of Knitting*. New York: Simon and Schuster, 1988. Veritable encyclopedia of basic knitting, but out of print.
Moreno, Jillian and Amy R. Singer. *Big Girl Knits*. New York: Potter Craft, 2006. Sizing for ample women's figures.
Square, Vicki. *The Knitter's Companion*. Loveland, Colorado: Interweave Press, 1995. Basic knitting techniques.
Stanley, Montse. *Handknitters' Handbook*. Devon, England: David and Charles, 1986. Basic knitting techniques.
Vogel, Lynne. *The Twisted Sisters Sock Workbook*. Loveland, Colorado: Interweave Press, 2002. Spinning and dyeing techniques.
Zimmermann, Elizabeth. *Knitting Without Tears*. New York: Simon and Schuster, 1971. Knitting for thinking knitters.

Tools
Hand-turned WPI gauge by Art Larsen
River's Edge Weaving Studio
Carol Larsen
348 East Front St.
Grand Ledge, MI 48837
517-303-0928
Weavingstudio@cs.com
Proportional Graph Paper
incompetech.com/beta/plainGraphPaper
tata-tatao.to/knit/matrix/e-index
Sizing and Measurements
knitting-and.com/knitting/tips/sizing
fiber-images.com/Free_Things/Reference Charts/standard_measurements

Index